Retirement
GPS

How to Navigate Your Way to
A Secure Financial Future
with Global Investing

Retirement

GPS

Aaron Katsman

Mc
Graw
Hill
Education

New York   Chicago   San Francisco   Athens   London   Madrid
Mexico City   Milan   New Delhi   Singapore   Sydney   Toronto

1 2 3 4 5 6 7 8 9 0   DOC/DOC   1 9 8 7 6 5 4 3

ISBN 978-0-07-181406-5
MHID 0-07-181406-X

e-ISBN 978-0-07-181407-2
e-MHID 0-07-181407-8

This publication is designed to provide accurate and authoritative information in regard to the subject matter covered. It is sold with the understanding that neither the author nor the publisher is engaged in rendering legal, accounting, securities trading, or other professional services. If legal advice or other expert assistance is required, the services of a competent professional person should be sought.

—*From a Declaration of Principles Jointly Adopted by a Committee of the American Bar Association and a Committee of Publishers and Associations*

The information contained in this book reflects the opinion of the author and not necessarily the opinion of Portfolio Resources Group, Inc. or its affiliates.

Library of Congress Cataloging-in-Publication Data

Katsman, Aaron.
   Retirement GPS : how to navigate your way to a secure financial future with global investing / by Aaron Katsman.
      pages cm
   Includes index.
   ISBN 978-0-07-181406-5 (alk. paper) -- ISBN 0-07-181406-X (alk. paper) 1. Retirement income -- Planning. 2. Investments. 3. Investments, Foreign. 4. Finance, Personal. I. Title.
   HG179.K3756 2014
   332.67'3--dc23
                                                                                    2013009004

McGraw-Hill Education books are available at special quantity discounts to use as premiums and sales promotions or for use in corporate training programs. To contact a representative, please visit the Contact Us pages at www.mhprofessional.com.

To my mother Tzivia, of blessed memory,
who longed for me to read. I can only imagine your
reaction if you had heard that I wrote a book!

Contents

Contents

....

Contents

Foreword

John Maynard Keynes famously quipped, "When the facts change, I change my opinion. What do you do, sir?" His words might well have addressed today's aging American, anxious in pursuit of a well-funded retirement and loath to acknowledge a world in which the once mighty United States no longer feels so mighty.

For those of us whose hairlines, waistlines, and bottom lines cruelly remind us that our youth is over, the memory remains of a time when, financially, the world beyond America didn't much matter. General Motors, Eastman Kodak, Xerox, Sears Roebuck, and their ilk were the Great Companies of the World.

They were, above all, American companies. The dollar was almighty. God wore red, white, and blue. And ever it would be.

In such a world, what red-blooded investor needed to look elsewhere? Indeed, in the 1960s and 1970s, long-term investment in a group of 50 large American companies, the Nifty Fifty, was considered a simple and fail-safe route to a robust retirement.

But along came the rise of Japan, the European Union, the Asian Tigers, and emerging markets, and lo! The Nifty Fifty were no longer so nifty, nor was the United States so singularly supreme. Products from companies with names like Toyota, Samsung, Novartis, and Nestlé became as ubiquitous as those from Ford, IBM, Squibb, and Hershey.

Further, all talk of future economic power turned to the juggernaut that is China or to the explosion of both populations and economies in such heretofore exotic backwaters as India, Turkey, Korea, and Brazil. To seal the demise of the Old World

Order, something called the Internet came along and shrank time and space.

As Dorothy said to her little dog after they emerged from their displaced shack into a Technicolor Oz of elves and witches, "Toto, I've a feeling we're not in Kansas anymore."

The facts have changed, sir. An American of today faces a global reality that he can neither escape nor afford to ignore.

But what's a graying American to do? How can he adapt his financial plans to this Brave New World?

China, Korea, India, and Brazil might well be on the rise, but how can one actually risk her money in such strange lands? Aren't these places rife with risk, instability, and corruption? One can't even pronounce the names of their currencies, much less invest in their economies.

Yet, if one confines his investments to the comfortable realm of our American homeland, he will surely risk suffering the pitfalls of investing in a nation that is mired in terminal decline. By so doing, he may turn our supposed golden years into years of penury and shame.

It's enough to make a grown man cry!

Fortunately, Aaron Katsman, a financial advisor who has made a career of helping his clients avoid such tears, has taken the time to write a book that will help retirees and those approaching retirement face a changed world with savvy and aplomb.

Writes Mr. Katsman: "In some ways, this is the point of my book: retirees need to eliminate the emotion of home bias and look objectively at the world's investment opportunities."

This simple but vital insight propels all that follows and sets the tone as well: folksy wisdom laced with entertaining stories, combined with a broad knowledge of world economies and their myriad financial products to paint a clear picture of how one can skillfully diversify his investments beyond the United States into what Mr. Katsman calls the GPS portfolio.

Among the significant themes in the book is the notion that a retiree should focus not on investment performance versus established benchmarks, but rather versus his own objectives and needs. The result is that one may make use of readily available global investment products to build a coherent portfolio that not only exploits the opportunities that can be found the world over, but also serves his own particular needs, be they income generation, capital preservation, capital growth, or a limiting of volatility.

Evidence of Mr. Katsman's honesty and conviction abounds. Though he himself is a financial advisor, he generously lays out ways in which investors might best avoid or limit the very services that he offers. Similarly, he did not shy from asking this bottom-up value investor to write a foreword to a book about an investment approach that optically flies in the face of bottom-up investing.

Is this a man looking to render himself unemployed?

Hardly.

Good sense has many faces, and this book is nothing if not an easy-to-read compendium of good investment sense for today's retiree or near-retiree. Though not an advertisement for financial services, absorbing its lessons makes it clear that for many, employing the services of a skilled financial advisor will be worth its weight in gold, if not dollars.

On a personal note, I have had the pleasure of knowing Mr. Katsman for a number of years. It is deeply satisfying to see his straightforward, expansive, and sensible nature expressed in print for the benefit of others. For the prospective reader, the result of taking a few hours to delve into *Retirement GPS* may well be the difference between a disappointing financial future and one that will ensure a secure retirement.

Now who would say no to that?

Nadav Serling
Jerusalem, January 2013

Acknowledgments

"Silent gratitude isn't very much to anyone."
—Gertrude Stein

I learned the hard way a long time ago that when you start thanking people publicly, you are inevitably going to forget someone, and he is going to be ticked off for a very long time. Well, I will play with fire and publicly thank some people who played a very instrumental role in the publication of this book.

My first shout-out goes to Zack Miller, the one who lit the fire under me to write this book. His friendship, encouragement, and mentoring throughout the process is hard to describe in words. I thank you, Zack, for actually answering my incessant e-mails and phone calls seeking advice. I will continue to value your insights, something that, as you know, is quite rare, and I hope that we can collaborate on some kind of project in the future.

I'd like to thank Tamela Rich for all her encouragement and her hard work in getting this book published. Her advice, critical eye, ability to make me stay focused, and ability to listen to my 20-minute soliloquies have earned my respect. Without you, I never would have seen Charlotte, North Carolina. Your part of this book is well deserved.

I'd like to thank all those who were willing to be interviewed. I thought I knew it all until I spoke with you. Your insight and openness were a big part of writing the book and had a profound impact not just on the finished product, but on how I actually advise my clients.

Speaking of my clients, their challenging of my concepts has certainly sharpened my investment philosophy. I actually enjoy learning from you all, and I just want you to know that your expertise in various areas has played a very crucial role in how I view the world.

I owe a huge debt of gratitude to Jennifer Ashkenazy, senior acquisitions editor at McGraw-Hill, for her professionalism throughout this project. Thanks for putting up with my complete ignorance of the writing process. I still remember our first conversation, immediately after my softball team won the league championship. I was pretty excited about that, and then you told me that you were accepting my book. I must have sounded like a kid in a candy store! Hats off to the rest of the team at McGraw-Hill, especially Daina Penikas, senior editing supervisor for making this book what it is.

What can I say other than that my agent, Judy Heiblum of Sterling Lord Literistic, Inc., is a miracle worker. You got me a book deal! Your help through the entire process of writing the book, from its infancy to the finished product, was amazing. To Benjy Balint—thanks for hooking us up.

A big thank you to Tony, Juan, Monica, and the rest of the PRG team in Miami. We've been together for a long time, and I look forward to many more years working together. Those massive, chocolate-filled gift baskets can be sent throughout the year, not just for the holidays! What can I say but that without Andrea Mancini and Rachel Weiss, I would have closed my business long ago. Rachel, your sticking with me through thick and thin is something that I cherish and will never forget. Sandy and Yoram, thanks for encouraging me to go on my own and Doug for teaching me the ropes in this business.

In my educational upbringing, I was fortunate to have been taught the value of thinking critically. I got a lot of it at home from my parents, but I would also like to thank some of my teachers, Rabbis Rosenthal, Moskowitz, and Fox, for instilling in me the constant need to question.

A big thank you to my father, whose subtle encouragement helped me get to the finish line. Thank you for being a great father and a role model for what I can aspire to be for my children. Your knowledge and clarity of thought are second to none. Oh, and thanks for changing the channel for me all those years.

While it's fashionable to make fun of one's in-laws, if the truth be told, my in-laws are amazing. Their willingness to help out with a sick kid, a daycare pickup, or a host of other activities at the drop of a hat has inspired me to be a better parent. MIL and FIL, a big thank you. Just don't let it go to your heads!

I want to thank my siblings, Daniel, Rachel, Abe, and Deborah, and their spouses for their support throughout all the years. Your giving me a place to sleep, feeding me, and your insane knowledge and constant fight for what you believe in are much appreciated. It's awesome being the baby. Special thanks to my sister-in-law Hannah, who was very helpful with great advice that let me get this book off the ground.

To David, Rina, and Pinny and their spouses, thanks for the way you welcomed me into the family and continue to put up with me. Dvora, what do you say to a pan of lemon wedges for a book?

I would like to thank the Lord for truly allowing me to be blessed with a great family. Lots of hugs to my kids, Tzivia, Moshe Aryeh, Penina Chana, Yonatan, and Nechama Esther, for being such great kids. Thanks for being patient with me during the many nights I was absent, sitting alone in my office writing and writing. Just try hard, that's all I ask.

The biggest thank you obviously goes to my wife, Yael. She's truly a supermom and an even more super wife. Your holding down an intense full-time job as well as being a very full-time mom leaves me speechless. I know I don't verbalize what you mean to me, but at least I can write it. You're the best, and I can't wait to continue life's journey with you.

CHAPTER 1

Matching Retirement Lifestyle with Retirement Income

When I was 10 years old, I got my first job; I was a newspaper delivery boy for the *West Seattle Herald*. There were probably 50 subscribers on my route, a manageable number for a kid to deliver to once a week. But the *Herald* wanted me to deliver an advertising supplement to about 500 other homes as well. I was a good boy and delivered the supplements for a year. I wasn't too keen on delivering the advertising supplement, and after a while I figured that I could get away with just delivering the subscriptions. Sure enough, that worked.

For about a month.

Remember, this was Seattle, Washington, which gets about 38 inches of rain every year but doesn't get enough sunshine to dry it up. After about a month of leaving the supplements in my driveway, you can imagine the pulpy mess that greeted my supervisor when she drove past my house. If you also imagined that this did not end well for me, you were right. I was fired from my first job at the ripe old age of eleven and a half.

What's that got to do with a book about retirement? It taught me the folly of shortcuts. I find that in life, if you follow the rules, you'll be okay. Retirees who invest in get-rich-quick schemes almost always lose everything; those who don't save because they intend to win the lottery almost always end up with nothing.

Why I Wrote This Book

Plain and simple, most of the books, advice columns, and radio and TV programs on retirement planning rely on outdated notions of what retirement means in the twenty-first century. Also, too few of the authors of these books highlight international investment strategies and vehicles. In advising a global clientele, I've found that international investing is key in achieving personalized retirement goals. More on that later.

While my retired clients span the globe, they seem to have similar goals and needs—helping their children, more travel, philanthropy, and enjoying their newfound free time. Let's start with what real people, not paid spokespersons for financial services companies, have to say about their goals and expectations. The 2011 SunAmerica Retirement Re-Set Study poll revealed the following:

- *Retirees have a new outlook.* Today, 54 percent of Americans view retirement as a new chapter in their life, rather than a winding down—a significant increase over the 38 percent that held a similar view a decade ago.

- *Retirement is being postponed.* Preretirees say that they now intend to delay retirement by five years—from 64 to

69—in part as a result of increasing longevity, along with the 2008 recession and newly projected financial need.

- *Retirement no longer means the end of work.* Almost two-thirds of those polled say that ideally, they would like to remain productive and include some work in retirement so that they can stay active and involved.

- *Financial peace of mind is now six times more important than accumulating wealth.* In fact, 82 percent name it as their key financial goal.

- *Unexpected multigenerational family assistance has become the new retirement wild card.* Preretirees must balance their retirement plans with the possibility of their having to support aging relatives, adult children, grandchildren, and siblings. Nearly half of Americans 55 and older expect to be providing this support and, in a new twist on child-care, 70 percent of those believe that their adult children will need financial assistance.[1]

I am convinced that most people writing pre- or postretirement information have never sat with a living, breathing client. Nothing is personalized. There is no focus on the client's goals. Nothing is real. They assume that a generic retirement lifestyle of walks on the beach and exotic vacations is a universal aspiration.

What about the person who wants to spend as little as possible during his lifetime so that he can leave a legacy to a favorite cause or to his family? I have several clients who have achieved that goal.

What about those who want to see their financial contributions take root in people and institutions during their lifetimes and who don't care to endow anyone after their death? I've helped people bring this to fruition, too.

I find that celebrity financial gurus dish out irrelevant information about going after returns that outperform market benchmarks when they should be helping people balance their retirement lifestyles with their retirement incomes. Anyone who doesn't take this approach is pitching products, not practicing financial planning.

"Wait," you say. "Outperforming the market is irrelevant?"

Yes, for most retirees it is irrelevant because what matters to retirees is financial peace of mind. The SunAmerica research backs this up.

The main financial difference between people who have retired and those who haven't is the source of their income. Retirees are funding their lifestyle choices with retirement income, and everyone else is funding their lifestyle choices with nonretirement income. No matter what your stage in life, you've got to balance your income with your expenses. That's playing by the rules.

The Biggest Financial Mistakes Retirees Make

I will set forth a new paradigm for a retiree's investment portfolio soon enough. Some of this advice you will embrace, and other parts you will ignore. Regardless of how much of your nest egg you decide to invest in the GPS retirement portfolio, I hope you'll avoid these top five mistakes that I see retirees make time and again.

Mistake 1: staying on autopilot. I recently met with a well-off American lawyer who was here in Israel visiting his children. He asked to meet with me because he wasn't happy with his investment advisor. His broker of many years had retired, and the new one he had been assigned to had never taken the time to get to know him. His now-retired broker had made a practice of calling the busy lawyer with interesting ideas and both portfolio and market updates, and he missed that kind of personal service. The lawyer was also disappointed with his investment returns and thought that his portfolio should have performed better based on the market's performance during the same period. When I asked him why he hadn't transferred his account to a different firm, he said that he was very busy and hadn't had the time to get around to it.

Investors need to stop running on autopilot. They need to take control and make sure that their money is working efficiently. This doesn't mean that you have to become a do-it-yourselfer; instead, keep in touch with your advisor on a regular basis to make sure your investments are doing what they are supposed to be doing.

Mistake 2: lack of organization. Too often, I learn that retirees have multiple investment accounts with different firms, which makes it difficult for them to supervise and evaluate their investments. When a client has multiple accounts, her financial advisor should be sitting on top of her entire situation. The professional should not just focus on one account, but rather should assess everything and see how the client's entire financial situation fits her goals and needs. In short, your financial advisor should be like a corporate chief financial officer (CFO).

Mistake 3: budgeting. I volunteer for an organization that helps get people out of debt. I can't tell you how many times I sit with someone and he tells me that he earns $5,000 a month and spends $5,000 a month, but for some reason he is always in debt. Nine times out of ten it is because he forgot about annual expenses when he formulated his monthly budget. Annual items could be car insurance, a vacation, or anything else that isn't a day-to-day expense, including home maintenance. When budgeting, always remember to take annual expenses into account. To help you with your monthly and annual budgets, I've included a budget worksheet in Appendix A.

Mistake 4: keeping too much in money market funds. Part of any financial plan is to keep enough funds to cover between three and six months of expenses on the side, totally liquid, in case of an emergency. This is generally referred to as an emergency fund. I often see investors keep more and more money in money market funds. While seven years ago money market funds were used as a strategic asset because they carried a decent yield, now they pay virtually nothing. Nada, as we say in the vernacular. Keep your emergency fund in the money market, but get the additional money invested and starting to work for you.

Mistake 5: locking assets outside your own reach. As retirees age, they usually don't add someone to the account who can make changes on their behalf. I advise retirees to give a child or a trusted relative trading authority. This way, if they are not able to fully supervise the account, it doesn't become frozen. There are many ways to go about this that provide for checks and balances. Perhaps you will want to require two signatures from a list of three possible signers. Perhaps you will draw up a power of attorney. Consult with your family and your advisors to devise a plan and instruments that work for you.

Funding Your Life Goals

No matter how you're funding your retirement—whether from investments, rents, royalties, pensions, or government assistance—you've got the same issue of balancing income and expenses in retirement that you had during your working life. Sure, you have different goals and constraints in retirement than you had in earlier phases of your life, but the need to fund your life goals is constant.

Far too often, financial planning conversations are centered on investing when they should be focused on funding your life goals. Clients and prospective clients call me all the time asking if they should invest in this fund or that opportunity, and at first they're surprised when I confess, "I don't know." The reason I don't know whether a particular investment is a good choice for the client is that most clients haven't defined their life goals. They come to me with account statements and ask me what to do with their money instead of telling me what they want to do with their lives and asking how to fund the journey.

How Much Money Do You Need in Order to Retire?

The amount of money you need in order to retire is based on how much you'll be spending in retirement, plain and simple.

It's a great maxim of many financial planners that, if you play your financial cards right, you will need less income to live in retirement. They reason that once you've retired, you don't have to commute to work, pay as much in income taxes, fund your children's college educations, or make mortgage payments. My experience is that most people need a nest egg that will provide the same amount of income in retirement as before, even if the categories of expenses have changed.

How can this be? Take a look at some of the life events that may happen during your retirement:

- Your home may be paid for by the time you retire, but you still have to maintain it, and you may have to remodel it someday because it's run-down or to accommodate a wheelchair.

- Your adult children need financial help. The SunAmerica study showed that 70 percent of respondents anticipated that they might need to provide some level of financial assistance for their adult children. Sometimes this means that the adult children move back in with their parents and bring the grandchildren along.

- Your parents need financial help. We're living longer, after all.

- Your medical expenses increase.

- You need to move out of your home into a more expensive residence where your medical needs are better served. Or perhaps you need skilled care in your own home.

- A cause that's important to you needs financial help.

- Your grandchildren deserve some spoiling. Or perhaps they need a college education that their parents can't afford.

- Your nest egg loses value.

- You want to do more with your golden years than sip coffee at your own kitchen table. If you want to have your coffee at a coffee shop every day, you've got to pay the barista.

- You lose a life companion. Now you must dig deeper into your wallet when you seek companionship by going to movies or learning a new hobby.

In spite of the Great Recession, some people haven't gotten the message that you can't live beyond your means. Here's a case in point. A retired couple from the American Midwest called to inquire about hiring me as their financial advisor. It soon became apparent that we were not a good fit. They had lost two properties in foreclosure, and they carried tons of credit card debt despite their ages (late sixties and early seventies). They told me that they had turned over a new financial leaf and wanted to start saving, even if it was only a couple of hundred dollars a month.

When I asked what they intended to do about their high-interest credit card debt, they said that they would default on it. I told them that they had an ethical duty to repay at least the principal to the credit card companies: "You took the money; you have an obligation to pay it back."

FIND YOURSELF IN ONE OF THESE STORIES

Ask yourself which of these options feels right to you. Most people want to blend these options a bit, but one will resonate overall.

- I want to save as much money as possible to leave to the next generation (save now to endow after death).

- I want to use my money during my lifetime to support the next generation (give while living).

- I want to enjoy things during retirement that I couldn't enjoy during my working life and still leave something behind for others (enhance my standard of living and leave something behind).

- I want to race my money to the grave and leave only enough to bury my corpse (spend now).

You need to listen to that little voice that says "yes!" to one of these options. Sometimes it helps to find yourself in a story, so here are four that illustrate the options just given.

Save Now to Endow After Death

Electrical engineers Aadi and Vanita live in a Boston, Massachusetts, suburb. With the exception of Vanita's 10-year hiatus while she was nurturing their two preschool children, they worked for the same company for nearly 40 years and are 3 years into retirement. They are fortunate to have both a defined-benefit pension and a 401(k), but the company has discontinued health insurance for retirees. Their children are married with families of their own; they are financially self-sufficient and will receive the proceeds of the couple's life insurance policies.

In addition to a mortgage-free home and $125,000 in savings, Aadi and Vanita own an apartment building that is currently valued at $5 million, but with a commercial loan balance of just under $2 million that is due in the next two years. The property generates sufficient income to pay the balance of the loan. Through a planned giving program, they have pledged the building to an organization that builds medical facilities in rural communities in India. The agreement includes a provision that up to $500,000 of the value can be diverted to their needs, but they are committed to leaving the entire value with the charity. They spend their time helping this organization reach out to other Indian expatriates who are in a financial position to help with its humanitarian work. This involves a moderate amount of travel, which they enjoy.

Aadi and Vanita have enough income to live comfortably in retirement, but Aadi's recent heart attack has made the couple appreciate the need to allocate some of their retirement nest egg to cover healthcare expenses throughout the rest of their lives.

Give While Living

Lincoln and Doris have been blessed with six children, all living near their parents in Charlotte, North Carolina. Since their children and now their grandchildren have always been the center of their lives, they want to provide for them as best they can during their retirement. When one of the kids needs orthodontics, her grandparents pick up the tab. Sundays are always spent around the large dining room table, and the grandchildren are now spilling over into the family room at card tables. Lincoln and Doris never miss a grandchild's dance recital or soccer game, and they plan to take each grandchild on a trip to a foreign country of the child's choice to celebrate his high school graduation.

Doris who is 62, is a medical social worker at a hospital and would like to reduce her hours significantly; Lincoln is an accountant, but not a partner in the firm, and at age 64, he is ready to retire. They will spend about $60,000 on themselves and their family yearly. While they have social security benefits of $35,000, they must make up the difference from the $1 million in their IRAs and 401(k)s. This means a balancing act of capital preservation and lifestyle choice so that they will not need to liquidate their paid-for home worth $500,000 for many years to come.

Enhance My Standard of Living and Leave Something Behind

Ruth lives in Indianapolis, Indiana, with her adult daughter. Her other two children are married with families of their own, but her youngest daughter, like so many other people the world over, has had difficulty launching her independent life.

While Ruth has been frugal for most of her life, seeing as she raised her three children with very little help from her ex-husband, she would like to improve her standard of living, once she retires. Although she has a small mortgage left on her home, she should have it paid off around the time she retires from her job as an office manager in a medium-sized business.

Ruth's living expenses are about $40,000 each year. Social security will kick in about $20,000, and she has an IRA worth $200,000 and another $200,000 in an individual account. She would love to spend time traveling the United States and enjoying time with her family. She wants to save as much principal as possible so that her children will be in a better position to help her grandchildren with the proceeds of her estate. She will have no life insurance after retirement.

Spend Now

Appliance salesman Richard and self-employed bookkeeper Nancy have raised their two children and put them through college, and they are now ready to retire and see the world. The high school sweethearts will qualify for their full social security benefit next year and have been researching countries that they'd like to retire to. Costa Rica may be the first one they try.

Their financial goal is to make sure that they have enough money to live on, estimating their expenses at $40,000 annually. Their savings are modest for retirees, a total of about $250,000 from savings, an inheritance from Nancy's mother, and small IRAs. Richard served in the Army right after high school and receives a small disability income for a bad knee. Their Portland, Oregon, home has a modest balance, and they are willing to live in a rental home if maintaining their home becomes a burden or if they need to liquidate it in the future to fund their lifestyle.

They will rent the house to others while they are living abroad, hoping that their rental income will cover the maintenance costs and taxes and contribute a little something to their cash flow.

Funding Retirement in a Global Economy

No matter which of these stories, or a combination of them, resembles your aspirations for retirement, the financial landscape is constantly shifting, like the earth's tectonic plates. Let's stick with that tectonic plate metaphor while we talk about investment strategies for retirement.

When an earthquake struck the east coast of Japan in March 2011, the entire world felt the consequences, whether directly through tsunamis or indirectly through interruptions in supply chains or higher sushi costs. Germany changed its nuclear power strategy. U.S.-based Berkshire Hathaway, which controls two of the world's largest reinsurance companies, suffered immediate "paper losses" of $150 million. While we may have political boundaries that separate us, capital, like the ocean itself, isn't as easily constrained. Retirees must consider the role of other markets and financial instruments, no matter what their financial goals. In fact, the U.S. market, as measured by the S&P 500 index, is only slightly higher than it was 12 years ago, and 12 years with no growth in a portfolio stinks.

This is not a book predicting the downfall of the United States; I am actually quite optimistic about future U.S. economic prospects. Rather, this book looks beyond the United States to include opportunities and instruments that are available around the globe. After all, according to an article in *Fortune* magazine, 15 of the world's 25 largest companies in the year 2011 were actually headquartered outside the United States.[2]

The growth rates of the Asian, Latin American, Eastern European, and even Israeli economies far outpace those of the United States and Western Europe. So whether you are speaking of Brazil, Singapore, South Korea, or Chile, the common denominator that these countries share is a young population, a growing middle class, political reforms, lower taxes, and policies that encourage entrepreneurship. As a result, we have seen strong growth for more than a decade, and that has been translated into very strong stock market returns and strong currencies. Obviously past performance is no indicator of future returns, but these trends are likely to continue.

Goals for You and Me

I remember back in fifth grade surprising my teacher with my answer to the traditional book report prompt, "Why did the author write this book?" As a natural-born cynic, I answered, "To make money." So now that I've met one of my goals—getting you to buy my book—I have two goals for you, readers.

First, I want to get you thinking about yourself. What do you like to do, and how would you like to spend your retirement years? While that may seem elementary, it may be more of a challenge than you imagine. If you have spent the last 30 or 40 years working and now you suddenly find yourself faced with years and years of free time ahead, filling that time in a way that will fulfill you is going to be more difficult than you may project.

Second, once you've determined how you'd like to spend your retirement years, the investment side of the book comes into play. Together, we'll figure out how you can pay for the retirement you envision through a portfolio that includes international investments. I advise a global clientele from my home base in

Jerusalem, Israel. With clients located across the United States and the Americas, Europe, Australia, the Middle East, and Asia, I have come to "live" international investing. I'm eager to take you on an investing trip around the world.

CHAPTER 2

A Fresh Approach to Asset Allocation

Thanks largely to the 24/7 news channels that need to spin non-news into "news you can use," investors are having a tough time cutting through the noise. It's easy to be misled by the talking heads who have to face only their editors and makeup artists, not real investors. Too many investors accept their incessant table pounding urging people to "buy and hold" and "stay in for the long term."

For the sake of full disclosure, I want to make it clear that I have an aversion to "conventional wisdom." I think it has something to do with my upbringing. My father always made a point of not swallowing anything hook, line, and sinker (he happens to be an avid fisherman!), but rather making sure that the generalizations that people make can withstand questioning and ultimately, like a good fishing boat, hold water. It's probably his training in physics and the scientific method that was behind this, but it greatly influenced me.

When I turned 13, I had a bar mitzvah, a Jewish rite of passage into adulthood. I had to give a speech, and my father helped me with it. Rather, I should say that he wrote it for me. I am not going to bore you with a lot of minutiae; it's just that the topic of the speech had to do with a Jewish holiday, Sukkot (the Feast of Tabernacles) and the size and amount of sunlight permitted for a sukkah (a temporary dwelling place where Jews eat and sleep during the holiday). My father found it interesting that our sages, who lived 2,500 years ago, used a mathematical formula similar to pi to make their calculations. My entire speech was challenging their approach and ultimately affirming that based on certain geometrical calculations, they were correct in using the formula they used. You see, you can't even trust a sage!

Why do I bring all this up? After nearly 20 years of sitting with clients, I find that those who followed conventional wisdom often suffered for it when it came time for them to retire. Buying and holding with a long-term perspective may be the right advice for someone in his twenties or thirties, but a 70-year-old retiree is in a completely different place in life. In most cases, retirees can't afford to lose 30 percent of their net worth when the market tanks, only to be told, "Hang in there; it will go back up."

A retiree's investment portfolio must be in tune with her goals, needs, and psychological makeup, of course, but it also must reflect the world of investment opportunities that are potentially poised for bigger returns than anything that is currently touted for a conventional retirement portfolio.

Investors, especially those who've been saving and investing for 20 or 30 years, are overly reliant on outdated models of asset allocation, which are "justified" by benchmarking to indexes and the use of Monte Carlo simulations. My approach will help retirees break these old habits and realize greater financial security.

If you are near to or into your retirement years, here are two ways to recover from the bruising of the Great Recession (or indeed any downturn): save money and cut expenses. Notice that I didn't say, "Make your retirement portfolio more aggressive." While this advice is for someone much younger, retirees too often follow it. They, not their financial advisors, and certainly not the talking heads on TV, are the ones who pay the price.

In this chapter, I'll show you what a conservative global portfolio strategy (GPS) retirement portfolio could look like and how over the last decade it has outperformed what the talking heads tout for retirees. And yes, I do so without exposing your precious retirement nest eggs to excessive risk. Before I can do that, however, I need to knock down some conventional wisdom in the areas of asset allocation and the "buy and hold" approach to retirement investing.

Asset Allocation and Diversification

In the story of the Tower of Babel,[1] the people of the world were united in their language and in their goals. In the language of the investment profession, this is *concentrated*. The Lord didn't like their motivations and ended up creating multiple languages and scattering the people all over the world. In investment language, this is *diversified*. If the Lord said that the best way for the world to conduct its affairs is in multiple languages and multiple geographies, then perhaps that's the best way to create an investment portfolio as well.

Okay, you don't have to be a Bible believer to see that investors who try to hit a grand slam by putting everything into a couple of stocks usually end up striking out. Can you say, "Tech bubble of 2000"? What about, "Real estate bubble of 2008"? It's true that if Bill Gates had listened to his financial advisor and diversified, he wouldn't be where he is today. Had he sold his Microsoft stock 20 years ago, he would still be well off, but he wouldn't be one of the richest men in the world. Unfortunately, for every Bill Gates, there are thousands of other people who tried this approach and ended up crashing and burning.

OWNING EVERYTHING

The flip side of being overly concentrated is "owning everything."

About a year ago, I sat with a prospective client who had an investment account worth about $450,000, held with a large, well-known U.S. asset management firm. As I was reviewing his holdings, what struck me most was the number of stocks he was holding. I counted more than 150 individual companies. I asked him how much he was paying in fees, and he answered 1.25 percent per annum. I couldn't believe it. I have no problem with paying fees if you are getting value added for your money, but to pay a lot and end up buying "everything" is silly. I explained that he could own a few mutual funds or exchange-traded funds (ETFs) that track market indexes and accomplish the same thing he is paying 1.25 percent for, for a fraction of the cost.

The reason that he went to this well-known firm was because he (and it) believed that buying and selling individual stocks is an effective way to build wealth; that's very reasonable, but shame on the people at the firm for marketing themselves as professional stock pickers, and then buying 150 stocks. For the 1.25 percent fee, they should be investing in what they truly believe in, not investing in trying to cover their behinds.

So far we've discussed diversification, which refers to investing in more than one instrument. Our discussion isn't complete without also addressing *asset allocation*, which refers to the classes of assets you can choose among. Broadly speaking, asset classes are equities, fixed income, and cash equivalents. Putting it all together, an investment portfolio is allocated among different classes of assets; it is diversified within each class of assets.

Asset allocation can help your portfolio achieve lower volatility, which provides it with more stability over the long run. Volatility measures the ups and downs in a security or portfolio's value. High volatility means that the price can vary significantly over a short period of time; conversely, low volatility means that there aren't dramatic changes in price; they occur at a slower and steadier pace. Low volatility is like the carousel at the county fair; high volatility is like the roller coaster. If you are properly diversified, something in your portfolio may drop, but your overall portfolio will benefit from gains elsewhere.

Keep in mind that neither diversification nor asset allocation ensures a profit or guarantees against loss. The question is how to allocate and diversify your assets, and this is where the GPS portfolio differs from what I'll call *classic asset allocation*. For those who are approaching retirement or are already retired, classic asset allocation generally advises a portfolio like this (where, unless something is specifically identified as "international" or "emerging markets," it is from the United States):

- 25 percent large-cap stocks

- 10 percent mid-cap stocks

- 10 percent small-cap stocks

- 5 percent international stocks

- 0 percent emerging markets stocks

- 40 percent intermediate bonds

- 10 percent short-term bonds

This type of model portfolio has generally returned 7 percent annually for 10 years and 4 percent annually for 5 years.

My GPS portfolio looks more like this in 2013:

- 10 percent large-cap core

- 5 percent mid-cap core

- 10 percent small-cap core

- 7 percent international developed markets

- 18 percent international emerging markets

- 10 percent intermediate bonds

- 8 percent intermediate municipal bonds

- 7 percent high-yield bonds

- 25 percent international bonds (includes emerging markets bonds)

And how does this portfolio compare to its benchmarks? Have a look at the performance summary in Figure 2.1.

This performance summary is based on 10 years of backtesting.[2] ETFs and mutual funds were used for asset classes to use in the test. The backtested results were achieved through the retroactive application of a model that was designed with the benefit of hindsight. The trades during the backtesting were not actually executed—they are simulations. These simulations cannot reflect all the complexities of actual investing, and there are many material factors, including those relating to the markets in general, the impact of fees and expenses, and liquidity activity, any or all of which might have adversely affected the actual performance.

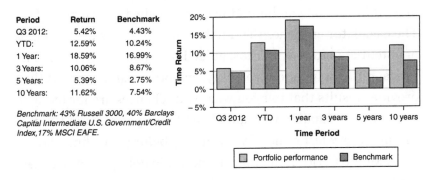

FIGURE 2.1 Performance Summary

Performance Versus Benchmark as of 9/30/2012

Period	Return	Benchmark
Q3 2012:	5.42%	4.43%
YTD:	12.59%	10.24%
1 Year:	18.59%	16.99%
3 Years:	10.06%	8.67%
5 Years:	5.39%	2.75%
10 Years:	11.62%	7.54%

Benchmark: 43% Russell 3000, 40% Barclays Capital Intermediate U.S. Government/Credit Index, 17% MSCI EAFE.

So there. You can follow what I'm thinking about the world on my website at http://gpsinvestor.com/.

I'll explain the GPS portfolio later, but first, we need to knock down some more barriers that the conventional media and financial institutions have placed between investors and the profits that could await them if they held 50 percent of their portfolio in international stocks, bonds, and cash equivalents.

Monte Carlo Simulation and Classic Asset Allocation

Monte Carlo simulation is a statistical tool that can be used to predict the outcome of everything from tornadoes in Kansas during July to the attitude control of the *Mars Express* orbiter.[3] In investment modeling, Monte Carlo simulation estimates the chances that you will hit your retirement goals given a specific set of investments.

How does it work? The investor enters information about his age, income, various assets, retirement-plan contributions, investment mix, and other financial details. You can also plug in the fact that you plan on marrying off two children, buying a new car every five years, and taking a trip around the world. The more information you input, the more detailed your plan will be. The calculator crunches the numbers on hundreds or thousands of potential market scenarios, guided by assumptions about historical returns, inflation, volatility, and other parameters. It then provides results that tell you what your chances are for living to a certain age, funding your anticipated lifestyle, and not running through every last dime of your money before your final day.

A Monte Carlo simulation of a portfolio does provide a decent service. It gives you a blueprint for trying to hit your retirement goals, and it's based on the results of a thousand or more possible scenarios. However, there are two problems with the system itself and a major problem with how it's used by both investors and their advisors.

Crashes. At the end of the simulation, the investor is told, for example, "You can feel comfortable that you'll meet your retirement goals with a success rate above 70 percent." However, the problem is that while the 1,000 or more scenarios do include some crash scenarios, once there is a real-life crash that affects your real-life portfolio, what can you do?

Historical data. Let's say the simulation is based on the investor's portfolio, which has 50 percent U.S. large-cap stocks and 50 percent U.S. government bonds. Starting with the equity side, this retiree isn't sufficiently exposed to non-U.S. markets, which is a problem, and what the foreign exposure there is tends to be focused more on Europe and less on Asian and emerging markets. As I will discuss in more depth later, some of these markets, which have produced much higher returns than their U.S. counterparts over the last decade, didn't even exist as investment destinations 100 years ago. Most model portfolios are underexposed to these opportunities. This is a shame for investors, as these markets have generated much higher returns, which you'll see as you read the rest of the book. On the bond side, the simulation is based on historical data where the yield was more than 6 percent a year, and in the past four years alone, we have seen that bonds are not yielding anywhere near 6 percent. Their yields are near zero. This simulation suggests that of a $600,000 portfolio, $300,000 should be in bonds. The simulation would say that this $300,000 would generate $18,000 in income, but in reality it would generate closer to $6,000, which misleads the retiree into thinking that she will be able to generate a lot more income than she will actually achieve.

Overreliance. There is a problem with using Monte Carlo simulation that has nothing to do with the simulation itself, and that's overreliance on its findings. Here's an example. Let's say that yesterday you met with your advisor to allocate your portfolio based on your goals and aspirations for the next 10 or 15 years of retirement with your family. The Monte Carlo simulation revealed that, yes, indeed, the instruments your advisor recommended would get you there. Skip ahead three months and your sister calls with an offer to go in on a condominium in Hawaii. A property management firm will lease the property for the weeks you and your family aren't using it. You go for it. Two years later, you're sitting in the doctor's office at the rehabilitation clinic, and you learn that to recover from her stroke, your wife will require a significant commitment to physical therapy and a home health aide that is not covered by your insurance. What with one thing and another, your portfolio's allocations will need to be revised because their underlying assumptions are history. This is a stark demonstration, but it makes the point that investment allocations, like any plan, need to be revisited regularly.

While your advisor is required to meet with you once a year to review your portfolio, it is up to you to look at the changes that have taken place in your life since your last meeting with your advisor, and bring them up at the next meeting. You shouldn't take false security from a Monte Carlo simulation's findings. As my favorite Beatle, John Lennon, said, "Life is what happens while you are busy making other plans."

Buy and Hold

"Buy and hold" is an investment strategy in which an investor buys stocks and holds them for a long time, regardless of market fluctuations. Conventional wisdom says that over a long time period, equities always outperform bonds and other asset classes. Following this worldview, investors take the advice that because you will never outperform the market, you should just buy indexes that track the market and never sell them.

Unfortunately, most advocates of this strategy ended up making no money over the last 12 years, which is what we call the "lost decade."

Zack Miller, author of *TradeStream Your Way to Profits: Building a Killer Portfolio in the Age of Social Media*, told me that investors can do well by mimicking smart investors instead of buying and holding. "You don't have to find creative ways to beat the market—for many of us, that's a sucker's game. Smart strategies that ape the 1 percent of investors who can regularly perform well will also get us to the promised land of profits." Miller quotes a seminal research piece[4] that showed that investors could come close to the returns Warren Buffett gets in his own portfolio merely by copying his filings with the SEC.

Miller offers another example, Joel Greenblatt, who put up amazing returns for 20 years and shared his secrets in *The Little Book That Beats the Market*. Someone once asked him why he's giving away the special sauce and whether his public revelation of his methods would interfere with his techniques. He replied that he wasn't afraid that everyone would adopt his techniques because individual investors have an extremely hard time sticking to an investment strategy. "They'd rather play investor cowboy than to implement a rigorous buy/sell methodology," he explained.

Mike Dever, founder and CEO of Brandywine Asset Management, had this to say about buy and hold:

"In 1999, global stock markets were at the peak of an 18-year secular bull market. Buy and hold had become a mantra. That's no big surprise. By definition, selling at any time prior to the peak would have resulted in less profit than having simply held until that peak. But that shouldn't have been construed as a revelation or the basis for an investment strategy. It was simply an observation. Yet books, articles, and investment seminars by the truckload were produced that expounded on the benefits of buy and hold. Buy and hold became one of the most dominant of investment myths.

"But the reality is that buy and hold is not a viable investment strategy at all; it is merely a way to rationalize losses. Let me explain.

"You may notice that financial professionals espouse buy and hold for U.S. equities, but not for those of Egypt, Mexico, Turkey, or numerous other countries. The reason has to do with survivorship bias. Of the (at least) 36 stock exchanges that existed in 1900, fully half have suffered at least one major hiatus in trading. Buy and hold wasn't an option for investors in those markets. Because the U.S. market survived uninterrupted over that period, it was one of the few that could even be considered for buy and hold.

"But the United States was a very different country in 1900 from what it is today. Its GDP was $20 billion. It was an emerging economy. Today its GDP is more than $15 trillion. Just because it proved beneficial to buy stocks for the long term in 1900 doesn't mean that it makes sense to do so today. Conditions are entirely different.

"Furthermore, those returns on U.S. stocks were very lumpy. From 1900 through 1950, the real (after inflation) return on stocks, even with dividends included, was zero. I can assure you that the vast majority of financial professionals were not espousing buy and hold at the end of that period. This was followed by a 50 percent gain over the next 32 years. It wasn't until the bull market fireworks started in 1982 that the 'real' returns were earned."

Benchmarking

If you ask the investing public to gauge how it's doing, it will invariably mention a benchmark: "I'm up 20 percent over the S&P 500 since last year." This works fine if you're a fund manager with a mandate to outperform the S&P. But what's your individual mandate for your investments? There's no question that performance is important, but I'd say the real benchmark is how your portfolio is doing vis-à-vis your goals and needs. Financial media will say that you have to keep up with your benchmarks, while I'm saying that it's more important that the retiree who needs to generate $20,000 each year get that much or more. For that retiree, getting more than $20,000 is "outperforming."

I had a client in 2012 whose portfolio had generated the low income that he required and who was preserving capital. He didn't want to take on any risk to speak of. His 25 percent in stocks was designed to keep up with inflation. However, the market had done exceedingly well in the previous six months, while he had made only 3 percent. He called me, claiming that he was underperforming the market and that he was very unhappy with his returns. I told him that he was comparing apples and oranges. His portfolio was all about capital preservation and income generation, not about aggressive growth and significant capital appreciation. Benchmarking tells people that they should be "keeping up," and that's not always the case.

For older retirees, it's not about making a killing in the market, it's about not getting killed there.

BUY AND HOLD VERSUS SLEEPING AT NIGHT

One of my clients just retired, and his portfolio is all the money he will ever have. In the midst of the euro crisis in 2012, he told me that on the one hand, he was very nervous that the financial markets would crater as a result of the events in Greece and Spain, but on the other hand, he "knew" that he should just sit on what he had because he "knew" that things would eventually get better.

I told him that the most important factor in all of this was whether he could sleep well at night. If he was scared about potentially losing a big chunk of his retirement money, he should lower his risk profile, sell stock, and move into cash until he was more comfortable.

If you tell that to a talking head pundit, he will trot out a slew of behavioral economists who will say that my client is making a big mistake because statistically he will sell at the wrong time, and then by the time he buys back in, the market will be much higher. That's an easy little editorial, telling people how they should act, but unless you are in that person's shoes (or facing her across your desk), you can't possibly know how she should react to the threat of losing 30 percent of her money.

The pundit may be right statistically, although I think a good advisor can help mitigate the bad timing issues. Many clients, like car engines, have "red lines," the level that they can't afford see their net worth drop below and the point at which they would need to sell. An advisor worth his fees acknowledges these red lines.

It's important to note that I am certainly not advocating that retirees become day traders. I just think that there is value to opening your eyes and seeing what's going on in the world. When there is a fundamental issue, sell.

The Global Portfolio Strategy Retirement Portfolio

I'm just about to reveal the rationale behind my GPS retirement portfolio, but first I need to address investor psychology, because the fear of investing in a region or country that you don't know well, you haven't traveled to, or whose language you don't speak is natural.

Investors have a "home bias," which means that they invest in what they know and are comfortable with. This plays to the fear of the unknown. Most models say that everyone should put 80 percent of his money in U.S. assets. European models call for 70 to 80 percent to be invested in Europe and 20 percent in the rest of the world. If you go to the state of Georgia, the most-owned stock is Coca-Cola, but is it any less risky than Pepsi?

The world is changing at an accelerated pace. Kingdoms, parties, and strongmen are being overthrown; economies that not long ago suffered hyperinflation are now models of equilibrium. By far and away the most dynamic and highest-growth economies are in emerging markets. Countries like Brazil, Peru, Chile, Colombia, Israel, Singapore, and South Korea have continued to show strong growth even with a slow global economy. Are you breathing yet? Don't worry, I am not some kind of maverick, Wild West advisor. I am not talking about investing all your money in Ethiopia or Vietnam. I'm advocating a balanced approach based on global growth trends.

Given this change, the obvious question is, how does one take advantage of all the global growth in an investment portfolio? The GPS retirement portfolio has about 50 percent U.S. exposure and 50 percent international exposure. The U.S. allocation is split among large-, mid-, and small-cap stocks as the core portfolio, and then I add U.S. sectors to the mix. The choice of sectors is based on both fundamental and technical analysis. I look for either sectors that are enjoying strong economic growth or sectors that have been depressed but look like they have bottomed out and are showing signs of economic recovery. Then the technical angle comes into play. If the sector stock performance has been lousy (corresponding to lackluster growth), but now things are improving, that's a sector I'd like to be in.

The global allocation in the GPS retirement portfolio is made up of both regional and country-specific holdings. It can be split among large-, mid-, and small-cap stocks and specific sectors as was done for the United States, with the caveat that there are not as many specific sectors to invest in globally as there are in the United States.

SECTORS THAT ARE POISED FOR GROWTH

I met with a client in 2012 who asked me what was interesting to invest in these days. He was expecting me to say technology, commodities, or Brazil. When I answered that I thought that regional banks in the United States were pretty interesting, he made a face and said, "Are you joking? The economy stinks, banks are going bankrupt, and it's their fault we had the financial crisis to begin with. Why on earth would you want to invest in them?"

There is no question but that this would be classified as a "contrarian" investment. Investors who go against the general market trend are called *contrarians*. A contrarian is also defined as an individual who believes that certain crowd behavior among investors can lead to exploitable mispricings in the securities markets.

For example, widespread pessimism about a stock can drive its price so low that it overstates the company's risks and understates its prospects for returning to profitability. Go back to the horrific BP oil spill. Every newscast was reporting on the total environmental devastation and suggesting that BP wouldn't be able to survive. The stock lost more than half of its value in a short time. During the crisis, I wrote that a contrarian investor would make the case that the company is the fourth most profitable company in the world, and that it's already lost more than half of its value. Even the worst-case scenario would mean that the company's litigation exposure and cleanup costs would come to maybe two or three years of its operating income. And no one would expect the company to pay up immediately; rather, much of the litigation exposure will be tied up in the courts for years. It was 19 years after the *Exxon Valdez* oil spill before the Supreme Court made a final ruling concerning Exxon's legal liabilities. I want to emphasize that this is by no means a recommendation to buy the stock—it's just a good example to explain the concept.

I am not recommending that you run out and buy regional bank stocks. This is what I would call "idea generation." You should research these stocks carefully before investing in them.

While buying and selling constantly and trying to time the market are not always advisable, it is worthwhile remembering that there are always opportunities in the market, especially after it has dropped. Analyze investments objectively without getting caught up in the hysteria and speculation that scares panicked investors and you can potentially profit when both common sense and fundamentals return.

Retirees who are living on a fixed income or an income generated from their investment portfolio face a daunting task. With interest rates so low, how can they generate enough income from their portfolio to meet their expenses without eating into principal? Let's say that you spend $70,000 a year and get $30,000 from social security. In such a case, you would need a portfolio of about a million dollars to generate the $40,000 (4 percent return) you need to supplement your income.

For the majority of retirees, this is far from realistic. How many people retire with a million dollars? Not only that, but in a period where you can earn only 1 to 2.5 percent on U.S. investment-grade corporate bonds, the 4 percent return assumed may be a stretch, and if you can get 4 percent, it will entail having to take some amount of risk by owning stocks, which in the event of a market drop could turn your million into $800,000. What is a retiree to do?

For individual investors who need increased income, it's time to start thinking global. Why not take advantage of a changing economic growth climate? If a 2 percent return is not enough to meet your needs, take a look at bonds that trade in foreign currency. While it used to be difficult to buy these bonds, nowadays most brokerage firms have the ability to purchase bonds in various currencies. For example, a highly rated (AAA) bond in Brazilian real can yield more than 8 percent. A similar bond in Australian dollars will yield more than 4 percent.

What makes these bonds even more attractive is that they are denominated in currencies that have been strong against the U.S. dollar. As a result, not only do you get the high interest rate, but you also have the potential to profit from the appreciation in the currency. If you can get a 4 to 8 percent interest rate and a stable currency, you are way ahead of the game, and you will be able to meet your retirement goals with even less than a million dollars in the bank.

But hold on, cowboy; past performance is no indication of future results. If the U.S. dollar gets stronger against the world's major currencies, you can end up losing money. This is why I am not saying that you should put your entire nest egg in these instruments, but rather that you should give yourself some exposure to them, as they can make a big difference in your retirement.

In the following chapters, we'll go for a trip around the world, looking for places to look for GPS portfolio investments, then we'll look at the investments themselves, and finally, we'll look at how to implement the GPS in your portfolio, either as a do-it-yourselfer or in collaboration with an advisor. But before we do that, I'll explain the rationale behind the GPS retirement portfolio.

CHAPTER 3

A Primer on International Investing

In Chapter 2, I let the cat out of the bag: I believe in investing 50 percent of a retiree's portfolio in non-U.S. stocks and bonds. How'd a guy who never set foot outside his home state of Washington for the first 18 years of his life become so cosmopolitan?

It started the day I flew to New York to study at Yeshiva University. I still remember my shock, as I went down to baggage claim at LaGuardia Airport, at seeing so many people of all nationalities, speaking a myriad of languages. I felt like a very small person in a very big world.

I majored in political science, but I enjoyed economics and I've always been a news junkie. To finish my degree in time, I took a summer course in political economy, which merges the two disciplines, at the University of Washington. I knew that this field was exactly what I wanted to do with my career, but I didn't want to become a university professor. And then it came to me that the best choice of profession was that of financial advisor.

Twenty-five years later, after extensive traveling, I am still amazed at how big the world is. And I am not the only one. I have clients who own companies worth hundreds of millions of dollars, and when they come back from a business trip they will often report to me, with youthful awe, what they've seen: "Aaron, we need to invest in Turkey. You can't imagine the economic explosion I saw there," or, "Aaron, I was just in Peru, and everywhere you turn they are building. It's just amazing."

Even around my office in downtown Jerusalem, a city that's known more for its spirituality than for its economic prowess, there is a big residential project going up right across the street from me, another two up the street are selling for a minimum of $550,000 (per unit!), and down the street from me are two large commercial projects in the midst of construction.

What's the point of all this? That, no offense to the United States, real and strong economic growth has become a global phenomenon. Let's go to Peru for a second, where the five-year compound annual growth rate is 7.2 percent.[1] That's off the charts.

As the global economic climate changes, investors need to change the composition of their portfolios as well. While the United States should continue to have decent growth over the next 12–15 years, experts predict that the other advanced countries of the world are going to chug along at sub-2 percent GDP growth. That's nothing to write home about.

Now, if you look at the growth trends for China, India, and the rest of the emerging world, their growth rates are about double that.

Take a Look Around

The strong global growth you see in Figure 3.1 is being driven by a burgeoning middle class. The OECD reports that over the next 20 years, the middle class in North America will drop both in numbers of people and as a percentage of the global middle class. The situation in Europe is much worse; its share of the global middle class is expected to drop from 36 percent in 2009 to just 14 percent in 2030. Contrast that to Asia and the rest of the world, where you see explosive growth in the middle class,

FIGURE 3.1 Global Outlook for Growth of Domestic Product, 2013–2025

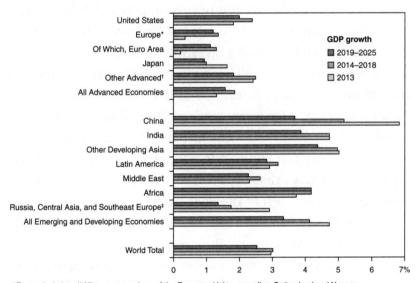

*Europe includes all 27 current members of the European Union, as well as Switzerland and Norway.
†Other Advanced includes Canada, Israel, Iceland, Korea, Australia, Taiwan Province of China, Hong Kong, Singapore, and New Zealand.
‡Southeast Europe includes Albania, Bosnia & Herzegovina, Croatia, Macedonia, Serbia & Montenegro, and Turkey.

Source: "Global Economic Outlook 2013," New York: Conference Board, November 2012, http://www.conference-board.org/data/globaloutlook.cfm, accessed January 7, 2013.

and you can clearly see that most of us will be living part of our retirement years during a major economic leadership change.[2]

According to a report from BlackRock Investment Institute, emerging markets now represent 86 percent of the world's population and 75 percent of the world's land mass and resources and account for 50 percent of world GDP at purchasing power parity (PPP), yet they account for just 12 percent of the global equity market capitalization on a float-adjusted basis.[3] This means that as emerging markets continue to grow, investors need to increase their allocation and exposure to these geographies.

Look at Figures 3.2 and 3.3, provided by the OECD. In Figure 3.2, you see the forecast for stunning growth of the middle class over the next 10 to 20 years. Almost all that growth will come from Asia. The United States will remain about even. Then in Figure 3.3 you see the amount of spending by the global middle class. It's this consumer-driven demand that makes for continued strong growth and intriguing investment prospects.

Investors who focus solely on the United States are making a flat-out mistake. While places like China, Indonesia, Brazil, and Peru used to seem far away, modern technology has made the world much smaller. With social media and advances in telecommunications, we can connect to people around the world. We often do so in ways that bypass traditional intermediaries like phone companies, such as Internet-based phone calls on Skype. Journalists themselves were bypassed by Iran's Green Revolution and the ensuing Arab Spring. Both of these events were brought to the outside world through Twitter updates featuring man-on-the-street photos.

This connectivity and sharing of information contributes to global trade by both driving consumer demand for products and facilitating the global supply chain. Take the iPhone, for example. It is a truly universal product. While it's engineered in the United States and manufactured in China (like everything else!), the

FIGURE 3.2 Numbers (millions) and Share (percent) of the Global Middle Class

	2009		2020		2030	
North America	338	18%	333	10%	322	7%
Europe	664	36%	703	22%	680	14%
Central and South America	181	10%	251	8%	313	6%
Asia Pacific	525	28%	1,740	54%	3,228	66%
Sub-Saharan Africa	32	2%	57	2%	107	2%
Middle East and North Africa	105	6%	165	5%	234	5%
World	1,845	100%	3,249	100%	4,884	100%

Source: Homi Kharas, "The Emerging Middle Class in Developing Countries," OECD Development Centre Working Paper No. 285, January 2010, http://www.oecd.org/social/povertyreductionandsocialdevelopment/44457738.pdf, accessed January 7, 2013.

FIGURE 3.3 Spending by the Global Middle Class, 2009 to 2030 (millions of 2005 PPP dollars)

	2009		2020		2030	
North America	5,602	26%	5,863	17%	5,837	10%
Europe	8,138	38%	10,301	29%	11,337	20%
Central and South America	1,534	7%	2,315	7%	3,117	6%
Asia Pacific	4,952	23%	14,798	42%	32,596	59%
Sub-Saharan Africa	256	1%	448	1%	827	1%
Middle East and North Africa	796	4%	1,321	4%	1,966	4%

Source: Homi Kharas, "The Emerging Middle Class in Developing Countries," OECD Development Centre Working Paper No. 285, January 2010, http://www.oecd.org/social/povertyreductionandsocialdevelopment/44457738.pdf, accessed January 7, 2013.

touch screen is from a Taiwanese company, and the processor is made in South Korea. Rumors have it that some Israeli companies are also supplying products for it, as is STMicroelectronics, and that a Swiss firm is providing the accelerometer.

Francis Fukuyama's 1992 book, *The End of History and the Last Man* made the case that free markets and capitalism are bringing about the "end of history" and are ushering in a new age in which the global economy will run solely on a free-market system and economic interdependence will bring security and peace.

Chung-in Moon, the brilliant scholar from the Republic of Korea, observes, "The confluence of the post-hegemonic world order and the triumph of capitalist market forces has advanced a new view of global peace and security in that the global spread of market forces and the decreased likelihood of major wars will reinforce a virtuous cycle of economic growth, prosperity, and peace and security."[4] What this means is that when everyone specializes in what it does best and relies on other countries to fill in the blanks, this interdependence will lead to peace and security.

Just keep in mind when you buy your next iPhone that you might be advancing the cause of world peace!

There are pundits who believe that economic growth in these boom countries is doomed because their economies are export-driven, and when global growth stalls, they will stall out as well; however, data show otherwise. The aforementioned OECD report on the growing middle class shows that there is a growing domestic consumer base in these countries, which translates into an economy that is much less reliant on exports. Meeting the needs of the exploding middle classes in these countries means that companies must ramp up production.

While this looks like an opportunity for large multinationals like Procter & Gamble, in reality, domestic producers will have a bigger advantage because neither American brands nor the need to "be more Western" is as strong today as it was in the past. There is plenty of room for domestic consumer staples companies to compete with the multinationals based in the United States.

There are plenty of studies showing that people prefer buying familiar, home-based brands. An NYU Stern School of Business study even showed that foreign brands are considered to be inherently more expensive than local brands,[5] and my experience from living abroad these twenty-some years is that they are.

CORN FLAKES ARE NOT UNIVERSAL

Advertising Age carried a story comparing breakfast cereals that demonstrates the power of local brands. Even as other countries adopt go-go Western lifestyles, they're not moving from their favorite breakfast foods to snack bars or ready-to-eat cereals. "Indeed, the toughest competition might be from breakfast foods that have been in place for centuries, like a watery rice gruel called congee in China."

I was fascinated to read that even when foreign consumers eat American cereals, they often eat them differently from the way Americans do. In Spain, for example, people pour their All-Bran cereal into their coffee. In France, people prefer Kellogg's Extra with yogurt, whereas elsewhere on the continent, people prefer it with hot milk. In India, Kellogg's plans to make Corn Flakes with saffron.

The Weakening U.S. Dollar

The typical American holds everything in U.S. dollars, whether it's stocks, bonds, or cash equivalents. While you may recoil from the possible risk you're taking on by investing internationally, you need to understand the nature of the risk you've already accepted by holding everything in U.S. dollars. Maybe it's because Americans have been spoiled as a result of King Dollar's reserve currency status, but if you travel anywhere in the world, the locals are sure to be holding more than just their local currency. Even the Swiss, who enjoy what is widely considered to be the strongest currency, don't hold everything in Swiss francs. Don't think that Europeans are free of home bias. When I was the head of international personal banking at Citibank, N.A. Tel Aviv, we opened accounts for clients in Europe. Citibank's model, which was similar to those of its competitors, was to overweight European currencies, equities, and bonds—the whole lot. In some ways this is the point of my book: retirees need to eliminate the emotion of home bias and look objectively at the world's investment opportunities.

The fall in the U.S. dollar is nothing new. In fact, the dollar has been slowly depreciating since the Korean War in the 1950s. I asked Cliff Wachtel, chief analyst of Anyoption.com and author of *The Sensible Guide to Forex*, if he thought U.S. retirees should have foreign currency exposure in their portfolio. "Absolutely," he said. "You need to diversify your income stream and assets by currency exposure, just as you diversify by asset and sector class. If history is any guide, then the Fed's unprecedented money printing is going to accelerate the USD's long-term decline against the other major currencies."[6]

Consider the following:

- Since 1970, the U.S. dollar is down about 75 percent versus the Swiss franc.

- Since 1990, the U.S. dollar is down about 42 percent versus the Japanese yen.

- Since 2002, the U.S. dollar is down about 38 percent versus the Canadian dollar.

- Since 1971, the U.S. dollar is down more than 80 percent versus the euro if we substitute the old German Deutsche mark for the euro, which didn't exist until the start of 1999.

Wachtel's right; the dollar's steady decline is an old story. Moreover, he believes that the Federal Reserve Bank's recent policy of holding down interest rates will accelerate that decline and the corresponding loss of purchasing power and wealth of any U.S. dollar–based investor.

While it is difficult to find any empirical reason for the dollar's behavior, and while theories abound, I believe that money has flowed into the local currencies of the main beneficiaries of global growth. This flow has made other currencies more stable, which means that fewer investors see the necessity of holding dollars. The dollar is no longer the world's lone safety currency. After being the butt of many jokes, the Russian ruble is actually a viable currency. Former president Ronald Reagan once said, "A strong currency is a sign of a strong country."

Enter the GPS Retirement Portfolio

For individual investors who need increased income, why not take advantage of a changing economic growth climate? If a 2 percent return is not enough to meet your needs, take a look at bonds that trade in foreign currencies. While buying these bonds used to be difficult, nowadays most brokerage firms have the ability to purchase bonds in various currencies. For example, a highly rated (AAA) bond in Brazilian real can yield more than 8 percent. A similar bond in Australian dollars will yield more than 4.5 percent.

What makes these bonds even more attractive is that they are denominated in currencies that have been strong against the U.S. dollar. As a result, not only do you get the high interest rate, but you also have the potential to profit from the appreciation in the currency. If you can get a 5 to 8 percent interest rate and a stable currency, you are way ahead of the game, and you will be able to meet your retirement goals with even less than a million dollars in the bank.

While I believe that if an investor were living in a vacuum (!), he should put all his money in emerging markets equities, close his eyes for 20 years, and then see how much money he made, I can't do that, and neither should you. Part of my job is to manage risk and volatility, and these factors go against the grain for retirees who can't afford a big short-term drop in their principal. That's why I developed the GPS portfolio.

Let's say I've convinced you that you should "go global" with a portion of your retirement nest egg, and now you want to know how to actually take advantage of all the global growth. There are three steps to this process. First, the GPS portfolio holds 50 percent U.S. and 50 percent international assets. Obviously this is based on the current economic and investing climate, but the international component is significant. You say you want to get your feet wet before you make the full 50 percent allocation? You wouldn't be the first to take that approach. It's very sensible.

Second, add sectors to the U.S. and international halves that are chosen strategically, canvassing the investment landscape for underpriced opportunities based on economic fundamentals. As I said in Chapter 2, I look for sectors that are enjoying strong economic growth and those that look as if they have bottomed out and are poised for recovery.

BEACON ROOFING

Back in 2010, hedge fund analyst Sammy Leibowitz (then working for Old City Advisors, LLC) gave me a great example of an underpriced opportunity based on economic fundamentals. This is a dated analysis, and I cannot advise holding this company (or not doing so), but I believe it illustrates the point about how to look for opportunities. He said:

"Beacon Roofing is a great example of a company that is in the right industry at the right time. Roofing makes up 86 percent of its revenue stream, roughly split between residential and commercial roofing. Within the $16.8 billion roofing industry as a whole, reroofing makes up around three-quarters of demand. This is crucial because buying a new roof is not a decision that a buyer needs to make; the decision makes itself. According to F.W. Dodge, an industry research group, only 11 percent of reroofing jobs are done to upgrade appearance. The rest of the jobs, almost 90 percent, are done out of necessity for reasons like age, leaks, or weather damage. Discussions with Beacon management reveal that the average roof in the United States is close to 20 years old, which is pretty much in line with the typical life span of a roof. So there is a lot reroofing demand on the way. This metric makes sense because the median age of the U.S. housing stock is 35 years, with around two-thirds having been built before 1970. For Beacon specifically, having a large Northeastern footprint allows this company to be specifically well positioned to capitalize on severe weather conditions. In addition, this footprint is growing. Since the company went public in 2004, it has gone from 66 branches to 208, mainly through 22 acquisitions. But there is still plenty of room for growth because it controls only 7 percent of this highly fragmented market. For example, only 5 percent of the distributors are regional. This is why it is likely that the company will only improve on its five-year compounded annual EBITDA growth rate of 9 percent and be in line with its projected 15 to 25 percent revenue growth rate going forward, with the stock price following suit."

This is research that I received at the end of 2010. Needless to say, the stock has had quite a move higher. Again, this is a great example of why investors shouldn't always be satisfied with buy and hold investing.

Third, there is a technical angle. If a sector's stock performance has been lousy (corresponding to lackluster growth) and now things are improving, that's a sector I'd like to be in. (See the sidebar in Chapter 2, "Sectors That Are Poised for Growth.")

The GPS portfolio model gives a tip of the hat to Dion Friedland, chairman of Magnum Funds, who observes:

The conventional approach to buying stocks and bonds is to study companies and industries and base investment decisions on fundamentals such as quality of management, strategy, competition, market share, company profits, and P/E ratios. A less conventional and more challenging approach is to make investments based not on these micro events affecting companies but on macro events.

Macro events are changes in global economies, typically brought about by shifts in government policy which impact interest rates which, in turn, affect all financial instruments, including currency, stock, and bond markets. Macro investors anticipate such events and shifts and profit by investing in financial instruments whose prices are most directly influenced by these trends.[7]

There are probably as many approaches to identifying and capitalizing on macro trends as there are macro hedge fund managers. This is beyond our focus.

The GPS portfolio is based on macro events and macro trends. As I revealed earlier, the GPS portfolio allocation is 50 percent to the United States and 50 percent international. Here are the macro criteria that I like to look at to help make a decision on whether to invest in a country or not.

Is there a stable political climate?

Is there a good legal environment in which corruption has been erased or is waning?

Is the country moving to free markets? Is it providing incentives for entrepreneurship?

Is the population young, and is there a growing middle class?

Does the forecast for the following year predict GDP growth with lower inflation?

Is the country's economic growth dependent on a single commodity, or is it diversified? A diversified economy is a better bet. Russia's dependence on oil and gas is an example of over-reliance on one sector.

Once you start comparing potential investments against these criteria, you can quickly discard countries that don't meet most of the criteria and still have a very strong international component in your portfolio. Remember what I said about sectors in rebound? The same thing works for international investing. A country that has lost 50 percent of its value but is showing signs of an economic rebound generally jumps to the top of the list for me.

There are dozens of approaches to identifying and capitalizing on macro trends, but they have two things in common: investing across multiple sectors and trading instruments, and seeing the entire globe as the playing field.

Let's use Colombia as a case study for how to apply the GPS model. We'll look at the rest of the world in Chapter 4.

Colombia and the GPS Retirement Portfolio

While it has been stereotyped, and rightly so, as a country where drug cartels run wild and are free to do what they please, Colombia has done a complete turn and not only has cracked down on the drug industry but has been moving more and more to a free economy.

According to Marketwatch.com, "In fact, the war with the FARC rebels is still simmering today, and the drug trade is likewise still active. But by strengthening its military and reducing bombings and kidnappings, and by going after the leaders of the drug trade, Colombia appears to have convinced foreign investors that the changes are here to stay."[8]

According to *Colombia Reports*, based in Medellín, Colombia posted GDP growth of 5.9 percent in 2011.[9] That's not too shabby considering the global economic slowdown. The economy is commodity-driven but is less reliant on mining and more focused on agriculture and energy, two sectors that may be primed for explosive growth. Colombia is producing strong growth in spite of a dismal global economy, and the country has done it by making fundamental changes in both its political and its economic system.

Remember what I said about youthful populations? About 40 percent of Colombia's population is under 20 years of age, and 80 percent is under 50. This means that we have a young population with a thirst for economic success and a growing middle class. This is the recipe for success. Note that there are many other countries in the world with youthful populations where there is not a growing middle class. If the two don't go together, I can't recommend investing there. There's nothing to rival a young, unemployed population with time on its hands to incite civil unrest.

Risks of Going Global

Some would call Colombia a "frontier market," so the term calls for definition. Let's define frontier markets by contrasting them with developed markets like the United States, Canada, and Japan. Frontier markets are often politically unstable, with poor liquidity, inadequate regulation, a lack of transparency, and a host of other issues. Investors are willing to accept the higher risks of these markets in exchange for the higher returns. More than one country has gone from boom to bust in a short time. Thus, investors have itchy trigger fingers, and if the miracle they expect from a frontier market doesn't materialize, they will sell and move on to the next market. This is another reason to like Colombia: its growth is driven by a fundamental change in economic philosophy. It reflects a cultural change, which makes growth more sustainable over the long term.

There are certainly risks with this type of investment. The threat of some kind of coup always exists in that part of the world. In addition, as the economy continues to post strong economic numbers and more foreigners invest, there is a threat of inflation.

The Securities and Exchange Commission has published a list of risks that investors should consider before investing abroad.[10] You can read its advice online, but I'll highlight those elements that resonate most with my experience and the experience of my clients.

- Sudden changes in market value magnified by foreign currency exchange rates.

- Political, economic, and social events that are difficult for investors to understand. This explains why brokerage firms hire analysts who specialize in geopolitical risks.

- Lack of liquidity as a result of lower trading volumes and fewer listed companies. Other factors are limited trading hours and restrictions on the amount or type of stocks that foreign investors may purchase.

- Lack of transparency. Many foreign companies do not provide investors with the same type of information as U.S. public companies. Even if they do, if the information isn't available in English, what good does it do you?

- Reliance on foreign legal remedies. Not only is it difficult to sue foreign countries in the United States, but even if you sue successfully in a U.S. court, you may not be able to collect on a U.S. judgment against a foreign company.

WARNINGS FROM THE SECURITIES AND EXCHANGE COMMISSION

Whether it's foreign currency trading, "prime European bank" securities, or fictitious coconut plantations in Costa Rica, you should be skeptical about exotic-sounding international investment "opportunities" offering returns that sound too good to be true. They usually are. In the past, con artists have used the names of well-known European banks or the International Chamber of Commerce—without their knowledge or permission—to convince unsophisticated investors to part with their money.

Some promoters based in the United States try to make their investment schemes sound more enticing by giving them an international flavor. Other promoters actually operate from outside the United States and use the Internet to reach potential investors around the globe. Remember that when you invest abroad and something goes wrong, it's more difficult to find out what happened and locate your money. As with any investment opportunity that promises quick profits or a high rate of return, you should stop, ask questions, and investigate before you invest.

The risks I've outlined can, to some extent, be mitigated by dealing with professionals. I have a client in Baltimore, Maryland, who came to me for international investing advice in 2005. Intellectually, he understood the need to invest abroad, but his portfolio was managed by a U.S. broker who didn't see the need to diversify outside the country. After the client sold his house, he took some of the proceeds and opened an account with me that was to be invested exclusively outside the United States. He wanted to start in small steps and compare the returns of the portfolios. Fast-forward to 2013, and let's just say that his U.S. broker isn't managing the size portfolio he was in 2005 because my client has been moving assets to places where they have been working harder for him.

I tell this story to assuage the fears of those who've never invested abroad. It may be scary at first, but the data do not lie: based on what we've seen, the world's strongest economic growth for the next 20 years will not come from the United States. Obviously, past performance is no indicator of future results.

Next, I'll take you around the world and show you how to put this primer to work in real regions, countries, and continents. On to Chapter 4.

CHAPTER 4

Around the World with the GPS Retirement Portfolio

Investor patience—all patience, really—is a virtue. Perhaps my love of fishing prepared me to hold hands with fidgety investors. You see, at a very young age, I was initiated into the Cult of the Fish. Maybe it was being awakened at ungodly hours on Sunday mornings to try to hook an elusive king salmon in Puget Sound with my father; maybe it was bicycling with fishing pole and worms in hand down to a favorite casting spot with my brother or a good friend to catch some sole. I don't know how much being at one with nature played into my eventual profession, but I'm sure the experience of waiting and waiting for the fishing pole to bend was excellent preparation.

Recalling those many hours on a boat with my father on warm summer days, without the urge to fill every minute with talking, many times listening to the late Dave Niehaus doing play-by-play on a Seattle Mariners baseball game, has a calming influence on me. When I get a client who always wants action by buying and selling and buying and selling, or when I start screaming at one of my kids (what can I say; I am human!), I think back to those days. In fact, my Jerusalem office has an enlarged picture of one of my favorite fishing spots.

THE OLD MAN AND THE SEA

I am about to let everyone in on a secret that previously only the members of my family knew, but I figure that more than two decades after the episode, doing so shouldn't get me into any trouble. When I was in sixth grade, I chose to read *The Old Man and the Sea* by Ernest Hemingway for a book report. I chose it for two reasons. First, it was really short, like less than 100 pages (no pictures, unfortunately, but you can't win them all!). Second, it was about fishing. I totally related to the protagonist, Santiago, as he kept going out to catch fish with no luck, never giving up even in the face of constant ridicule. Like Santiago, I was ridiculed by a sister, who cheered that "the fish won" when I came home empty-handed.

So what's the big secret, you ask? Well, let's just say that I became a minor expert in the book because I managed to write a book report on it every year for the following seven years in a row, including my freshman year in university. Until now, who was to know?

In a little piece of irony, I am actually writing this story sitting in a Starbucks in Seattle on vacation, looking out across Puget Sound to Bainbridge Island, the site of my biggest catch ever, a 16.5-pound king salmon!

*All the world is a very narrow bridge, and the
most important thing is not to fear at all.*
—Rabbi Nachman of Breslov

When I explain to clients and prospects the need for a lot more exposure in international markets, I am usually met with a bit of fear. I always caution that I am not talking about investing as if it's the Wild West. The GPS retirement portfolio assumes a measured and well-reasoned approach to looking at long-term global economic trends and taking advantage of a new economic reality.

When it comes time to actually implement the GPS retirement portfolio, many clients prefer doing it in stages. They say that they first want to get their feet wet before they jump in and invest half their money outside of the U.S. borders. While I believe in being patient with investors, investors need a bit of patience when it comes to investing abroad. Investing internationally, especially in emerging markets, can be more volatile, but it ultimately has the potential to pay off handsomely, as we have seen previously in the returns of my model portfolio.

In this chapter, we'll set out on a global tour to analyze which geographies are up-and-coming for investments; we'll also see which ports to just keep on sailing by and why. In this chapter, consider me to be like TV's "Julie, your cruise director" of *Love Boat* fame, using the classic introduction from ABC's *Wide World of Sports*: "Spanning the globe to bring you the constant variety of sport! The thrill of victory . . . and the agony of defeat!"

Because everyone wants to know about the shifting economic prowess of the world's superpowers, our worldwide tour starts with China, the world's growth engine. For those who are interested in China, the next question is usually about India. The two countries are similar because of their populations and rapid economic growth. However, while they are often grouped together, I think their situations are quite different, so I'll address them in turn.

China

Back in 2009, economist Larry Kudlow wrote, "*Fortune* magazine recently reported that the number of U.S. companies in the world's top 500 fell to the lowest level ever, while more Chinese firms than ever made the list. Thirty-seven Chinese companies now rank in the top 500, including nine new entries. Meanwhile, the number of U.S. firms has fallen to 140, the lowest total since *Fortune* began the list in 1995. This is not good."[1] Kudlow was writing from the angle of what the United States needed to do to get its economy back on track and regain economic superpower status. From an investor's perspective, however, investments need to mirror the global reality.

Chinese companies are growing fast, but in many ways they are taking on the competition and beating them at their own game. Take the auto industry. While the Germans and South Koreans gave Detroit and Japan a run for their money, the United States and Japan remained on top. But by 2010, the *Daily Mail* reported that China had become the world's largest automaker, partnering with all the global brands.[2]

With no capital gains tax and low corporate taxes, China has created a very friendly business environment. Within this environment, a new middle class has emerged, and it will probably be the largest middle class in the world in the not-too-distant future. The country's communist rule has produced what I define as full employment, with urban unemployment rates of around 4 percent. While the days of greater than 10 percent annual growth may or may not be over, conventional wisdom says that China will most probably become the world's largest economy in the next decade or two. Over the course of this book, I've explained my view of conventional wisdom, so let's just say I am skeptical about when or if China becomes number one.

Look back 12 years, to the time when China was hit with the killer SARS disease. Markets were crushed. I was with Citigroup at the time, and I recommended to my more open-minded (dare I say "adventurous"?) clients that they start building exposure to China into their portfolios. Back then there weren't a lot of ways to invest in China, so I recommended a J.P. Morgan China Fund. This was before the China trade became popular, and thankfully my clients made a boatload of money, some of them doubling or even tripling their money in a few years. Today there are several means and ways to invest in China. But should you?

That was then and this is now. In spite of all the success that China is enjoying, there are still potential roadblocks ahead. In the last chapter, when I gave the GPS retirement portfolio criteria, I mentioned that economic growth isn't the only thing I look at. I also look at political and legal transparency. This is where the outlook for China gets cloudy. Lack of corporate, governmental, and legal transparency makes it very difficult to tell clients to invest directly in China. According to the Heritage Foundation, "The judicial system is vulnerable to political influence and Communist Party directives, and corruption is perceived as widespread. The party's small leadership group holds ultimate authority, and directs control over many aspects of economic activity. The pace of genuinely liberalizing economic reform has slowed or stopped. The government has tried to counter the slowdown in global demand with expansionary fiscal and monetary interventions."[3] In layman's terms, start up the printing presses; let's print some money! This is very worrisome to me. Investors can never believe economic data coming out of China. Is growth really 8 percent and inflation 5 percent? Who knows? There are various agendas at play in the country, and transparency for investors is not high on that list.

You may say that economic data are not to be believed anywhere in the world. Even in the United States, during the 2012 presidential campaign, partisans claimed that the Obama administration had "cooked the books" to show a sudden, huge improvement in the employment picture to aid the president's reelection bid. Ahem. In the United States, economic data always come with revisions to previous data, and with those corrections, a clearer picture of the true state of affairs can be pieced together. China is not even close to that level of transparency and disclosure. Yes, some Chinese data are probably accurate, but who knows which?

Here are some examples of how to invest in China. In order:

1. We've been hearing forever that investing in U.S. companies with international operations is the tried-and-true approach. That's a watered-down exposure; the impact of their China business might be meaningless to the company's bottom line.

2. Invest in conventional mutual funds and ETFs. The lion's share will be local companies rather than multinationals, and thus you've got an issue of government's hand in the till.

3. Invest in a way that's aligned with the consumer (via new ETFs on the market), away from the government-owned companies.

4. The other way to invest in China is in the currency. It may be the safest vehicle as long as China continues to let its currency float with "water wings." (Water wings are those inflatable rings that children wear on their arms when they're learning to swim.) The Chinese government isn't

ready to throw its currency into the deep end of the pool with the rest of the world's currencies.

I have a decent track record with China predictions. Not only was I right about investing in China during the SARS crisis, but back when I was in university, I wrote a political science paper on social uprisings in China, and the next month the whole Tiananmen Square episode dominated the news. My professor thought I was crazy and gave me a B-minus, but I had the last laugh.

At some point, China may have a banking crisis that will make the 2008 financial meltdown in the United States look like a warm-up for the big event. The Chinese government has virtually forced all banks to lend more money in an effort to prop up the economy. Some local governments have been using the money to build unnecessary infrastructure, or, as we Americans call it, "bridges to nowhere," to boost growth.

When an economy continues to slow, politicians are tempted to apply even more government stimulus, leading to more loans that institutions will be challenged to repay. The communist government has been forcing banks to lend to probably bankrupt government-run corporations or entities for decades; these entities will never repay the debt. Doesn't this sound eerily like the subprime debt crisis in the United States? Giving mortgages to those who have no ability to repay them?

Change will come from social pressures, too. The *Economic Observer*'s deputy editor-in-chief, Zhang Hong, predicts that China's one-child policy could bring the country to its knees: "The direct result of a slowdown in population growth is an irrational demographic structure. China's population is aging so fast that it now has the '4-2-1' problem. When the only-child becomes a parent, he has to support two parents and four grandparents by himself."[4] While people around the world question how the

United States's social security and Medicare programs will remain solvent, the Chinese safety net of one child to six retirees is surely unsustainable.

Finally, China faces a major water problem, which might lead to civil unrest. As noted investor Jim Rogers said, "China has a huge water problem. In Northern China, they're running out of water. They know this and they're working on it, big time. But if they don't solve it or if they don't solve it in time, then China has failed."[5]

India

We all have a perception of India as an export-driven economy led by the information technology outsourcing sector. How many times have any of you called customer service and ended up speaking to someone in India? You can't even keep track of how often it's happened. Let's face it, other than Gandhi and food with lots of curry, the first thing we all associate with India is the outsourcing trend.

Let's dig beneath the surface, though. Boosters of India as an investment destination point to the huge role that its private sector plays in the overall economy; the government accounts for less than 20 percent of India's GDP.[6] This all sounds pretty intriguing, but there is another side of India that bears consideration: corruption.

Crony capitalism has enriched politicians and their friends and done nothing to bring basic resources like electricity to hundreds of millions of citizens who are in dire need of them. Take, for example, the recent $34 billion Coalgate scandal. The government's opaque allotment process apparently enabled well-connected businessmen and politicians to obtain rights to undeveloped coalfields. A member of Parliament may have conspired to fraudulently obtain five lucrative coal allocations.[7] I am not naïve enough to think that scandals like these never take place in other countries, but the commonplace nature of them in India concerns me as an investor.

Dr. Elliott Morss, an economic consultant to developing countries on issues of trade, finance, and environmental preservation, and manager of morssglobalfinance.com, a website that covers global economics and finance, is dubious of India's future, in light of its current culture of corruption: "I am not at all optimistic about India. It is a poorly functioning democracy, and democracy is most definitely not the appropriate form of governance for a society with ethnic groups that dislike one another. As in the United States, special interest groups will find ways to get the government to do things that go against the nation's interest but makes them lots of money. I see things deteriorating in India."[8]

The Heritage Foundation puts it this way: "The rule of law is uneven across the country, and the independence of the judicial system is poorly institutionalized. Judicial procedures tend to be protracted, costly, and subject to political pressure. Property rights are not protected effectively, and the enforcement of intellectual property rights is seriously deficient. Corruption continues to erode confidence, particularly in connection with government procurement and defense contracts."[9]

Sure, India is the world's largest democracy. It and China together have more than a third of the world's total population. Both have rapidly growing economies, and there are those who claim that first China will pass the United States as the largest economy in the world, and then India will pass China 20 years later. As I mentioned before, I am more than a little skeptical about that, and as for India taking the top spot, I think it would have to average 9 percent annual growth for the next 25 years to become number one, and I wouldn't put any money on that playing out.

While India is a democracy, it has serious geopolitical risk. At any moment, a war with Pakistan could break out over Kashmir, and as both have access to nuclear weaponry, who knows what the outcome of that dust-up would be?

India is a very poor country, and the gap between the haves and the have-nots continues to widen. India is about as far from a one-child policy as is possible, and the continued population explosion is being led by the destitute, not the middle class.

Two figures taken from World Bank research tell the tale. In Figure 4.1, you see the growth of GDP in India and China over the past 40 years, and in Figure 4.2, you see current socio-economic data for the two countries. At first glance, looking at these figures, you see how far ahead of India China is. To me that is what makes India a more appealing option. You have so far to go in building the basic infrastructure. And you can see the potential for a robust consumer-driven economic growth model, as the overwhelming majority of Indians lack the basic material goods that most of the world takes for granted, such as cell phones.

Sunil Asnani, a research analyst for Matthews International Capital Management, LLC, likes India's reliance on consumption, which contributes as much as two-thirds of its national income, compared to less than half in China's case.[10] But when I spoke to Dr. Morss, the India doubter, and asked him about the consumer being the ultimate driver of economic growth, he said, "Certainly India has a growing middle class that will spur macroeconomic demand. But recognize that India, unlike China, is already running a large current account deficit, making it a debtor to the rest of the world, which is unsustainable for a developing economy. And recognize that the growing demand from the middle class will be for Western goods and energy. How will they pay for them? An even larger current account deficit? And then there is

FIGURE 4.1 China and India, GDP (Constant U.S. Dollars)

Country	1970	1980	1990	2000	2010
China	180	183	445	1,198	3,246
India	120	161	276	475	973
China/India Differential	4,952	23%	14,798	42%	32,596

Source: World Bank

infrastructure that also requires Western goods. Unlike China, India has barely started to upgrade its infrastructure."

So I am writing a book about the need to invest globally, and the two largest and "hottest" global investing destinations aren't exactly getting the Katsman Seal of Approval. Have no fear, because we are going to stay in Asia, but we will focus on emerging Asia and the Asia-Pacific region.

FIGURE 4.2 Socioeconomic Data, China and India

Item	China	India
GDP per capita (current U.S. dollars)	5,430	1,489
Poverty gap at $2 a day (%)	10%	25%
Adult literacy rate	94%	63%
Life expectancy at birth, total (years)	73	65
Secondary school enrollment	81%	63%
Fertility rate, total (births per woman)	1.6	2.6
Access to electricity (% population)	99%	66%
Telephone lines (per 100 people)	26	3
Internet users (per 100 people)	35	7

Source: World Bank

Asia

While I may have come across earlier as being anti-China, I want to be clear that that's primarily in terms of investing, as there is no denying that it is the most populous country in the world, and that even if its growth slows, it will still be quite strong relative to the rest of the world and will help pull the Asia-Pacific region into continued economic prosperity. I like Asia-Pacific countries better than China as an investment destination based on some of the indicators that I mentioned earlier, such as transparency, a commitment to free markets, and an uncorrupted political and judicial system.

So when I say "Asia," I mean Asia without China, India, and Japan, but adding the Australian continent. With that definition, Asia is a place with very strong economic fundamentals, and for the most part the region came through the 2008 global crisis unscathed.

Asian economies are buoyed by rapidly growing populations, increasing consumer classes, and strong balance sheets. This is the direct opposite of the majority of the countries in the Western world, all of which show declining birthrates; struggling, debt-laden consumers; and budget deficits and long-term debt that could sink many of these nations.

The region is still predicted to post 6 to 7 percent annual growth over the next few years, well above the 1 to 2 percent that's expected from the developed Western world. While any continued slowdown in China could slow growth on the rest of the continent, I think that it would be muted because these economies are making the transition from being export-driven and selling to China to having an exploding middle class that earns and spends more money at home, too.

ASIAN TIGERS

Think back to the period from the mid-1970s to the mid-1990s. The investment rage was the Asian Tigers. Hong Kong, South Korea, Taiwan, and Singapore successfully transformed themselves from backward developing countries into cutting-edge leaders of the technology revolution. When you think of consumer electronics or new gadgets and toys, this region owns the space. Earlier in the book, I spoke about how the iPhone has done a lot to connect the world through sourcing parts from countries throughout the world. The biggest competition to the iPhone comes from South Korea's Samsung.

According to Nicholas Vardy, Chief Investment Officer of Global Guru Capital LLC and editor of *Bull Market Alert* and *Triple Digit Trader*, high-end, fast-paced trading services that focus on making short-term profits in the hottest markets in the world, "There is no higher-profile emblem of South Korea's success than consumer electronics giant Samsung. If yesterday belonged to the Sony Walkman and PlayStation, today belongs to Samsung's dazzling array of high-tech gadgetry. Today, Samsung has sales of $120 billion—more than double that of Microsoft—along with a reputation for making hip and sophisticated mobile handsets, MP3 players, televisions, and digital cameras. Samsung ranks ahead of Japan's Sony in televisions and trails only Finland's Nokia in mobile phones, recently having overtaken Motorola. Samsung's stock market capitalization, at over $110 billion, is more than three times that of Sony and is second only to Apple among consumer electronics companies."[11] I even bought a new Samsung flat-screen TV for my home, and it's awesome!

Hong Kong and Singapore have become major financial players. Because of the growth in their financial markets and the continuing flood of new regulations in the United States, investors have started to use these markets to bypass New York when raising capital. When it comes to raising money for initial public offerings (IPOs), Hong Kong has been locked in a battle with the U.S. exchanges. While Hong Kong had a bad year in 2012 because of a lack of investor appetite for Chinese shares and the massive Facebook offering in the United States, over the last 10 years Hong Kong has taken the title of king of the IPOs.

The main characteristics that all four countries shared as they climbed the economic ladder was investing heavily in education, encouraging savings, and emphasizing exports to richer industrialized nations, particularly the United States. As they have matured and a middle class has emerged, we have seen a spike in local domestic consumption. As I have said repeatedly, a growing middle class is what will drive continued economic growth.

If the United States relies on Asia, so should investors. President Obama said in 2012, "The United States is, and always will be, a Pacific nation. Many of our top trading partners are in this region. This is where we sell most of our exports, supporting some 5 million American jobs. And since this is the world's fastest growing region, the Asia Pacific is key to achieving my goal of doubling U.S. exports—a goal, by the way, which we are on track right now to meet."[12]

AUSTRALIA

This country has developed a model economic structure. It has pro-business policies, has plenty of transparency, and follows the rule of law. According to the Heritage Foundation's 2012 Index of Economic Freedom, Hong Kong, Singapore, Australia, and New Zealand take the top four slots. The description of Australia says it all:

"The foundations of economic freedom in Australia are strong and well supported by excellent protection of property rights and an independent judiciary that enforces anti-corruption measures effectively. While many large advanced economies have been struggling with growing debt burdens that result from years of heavy government spending, Australia's gross public debt stands at less than 25 percent of GDP. Budget deficits have been under control owing to prudent public finance management that recognizes limits on government.

Australia's modern and competitive economy benefits from the country's strong commitment to open-market policies that facilitate global trade and investment. Transparent and efficient regulations are applied evenly in most cases, encouraging dynamic entrepreneurial activity in the private sector."[13]

Australia is blessed with natural resources, and its strong economic growth over the last decade is due in part to its being a supplier of natural resources to China. While iron ore and other resources have led the charge, it looks as if Australian agriculture will be a major player in actually feeding the Chinese.

Chinese Citic Pacific Mining executive chairman Dongyi Hua said that "Australia has a golden opportunity to meet China's soaring demand for high-quality food" and he "would prefer to invest in agriculture rather than iron ore."[14]

ASEAN

Perhaps the most compelling subregion of this area is the ASEAN countries, of which there are 10. I'll hit you with the formal name once: Association of South East Asian Nations. The ASEAN countries are Brunei Darussalam, Cambodia, Indonesia, Laos,

Malaysia, Myanmar, the Philippines, Singapore, Thailand, and Vietnam. Many people, myself included, believe that they will be this decade's and the next's new Asian tigers.

According to a report on Asia published by the consulting firm Accenture, "By 2020, the region is expected to be among the world's 10 largest economies and the fourth largest in Asia. The demographic fabric will consist of more than 650 million people, most of whom will be middle class, educated and aged below 30, with rising disposable incomes and a strong appetite for consumption."[15] To quote Kramer from the TV sitcom *Seinfeld*, "Giddy up."

What, so you don't want to invest your hard-earned retirement portfolio in Brunei or Darussalam? (Ha, I gotcha—Brunei Darussalam is the official name of Brunei.) To be clear, I wouldn't dump my entire nest egg there, but I would certainly allocate some money to the six major players in this region, otherwise known as the ASEAN 6: Indonesia, Malaysia, the Philippines, Singapore, Thailand, and Vietnam.

I referred to Francis Fukuyama's book *The End of History and the Last Man* earlier in the book. He speaks about the need for countries to specialize in what they do best, then become dependent on other countries to fill in what's lacking. This economic interdependence will help lead to peace, I promise you, and the ASEAN countries are taking this to heart.

In 2011, the smaller ASEAN countries (Brunei Darussalam, Indonesia, Malaysia, and the Philippines) implemented an effort to collaborate in fishing and agriculture in order to increase productivity and lower costs in the greater region.

Japan

I love the Asia-Pacific region, and I think it is an intriguing place to invest. But there is one country I have left out. It's the country with the third-largest economy in the world, Japan. What can I say? Japan has problems that will take time to fix. The stock market peaked in the late 1980s. To say that the debt situation is a bit reminiscent of 2012 Greece is an understatement.

The Diplomat reports, "In 2011, general government gross debt totaled nearly 230% of GDP and is projected to reach 245% in 2013. . . . In comparison with Europe's indebted economies, Greece reached crisis point with its debt to GDP ratio of just 150 percent, while the Spanish government has faced a storm with a debt ratio below 100 percent."[16]

Japan is also suffering with an aging population. It's not that I have anything against retirees—heck, this book is for them. It's just that with an aging population, all kinds of benefits need to be paid as part of the social safety net system, yet there is no one to pay in to make sure that the programs are funded. Sound similar to the United States? I would much rather go with a country or region where a good chunk of the population is under 30. It's just a model for much more economic sustainability.

Latin America

In many ways, the whole GPS retirement portfolio strategy comes to fruition in Latin America. However, if you just start investing in anything Latin American, you'll miss out on the best opportunities for growth.

To understand how to invest in the region, you must understand the philosophical underpinnings that are at work. You have the Pacific Alliance (Mexico, Peru, Chile, and Colombia), which has expanded trade with the United States and Asia and posted strong economic growth. Compare the success of these countries with that of countries that have moved toward government-controlled markets and are on the verge of bankruptcy—think

Venezuela. J. J. Sussman, CEO of ActivePath, who spends a substantial amount of time in the region, told me, "Back in the '80s they used to compare Argentina to New York. That's no longer the case. When I am in Argentina, I feel that time stopped, and it's still 1986. Contrast that to Chile and Brazil, where everywhere you turn there is building and a general sense of vibrancy that is lacking in Argentina."[17] Then you have Brazil, which has moved toward free markets and become a rising star in the global economic scene.

BRAZIL

If I were to ask you to name a very populous country with strong economic growth and a growing middle class, chances are that you would answer China or India. While these are both correct answers, there is another country that also fits the criteria, and that is Brazil. When we think of Brazil, we think of a global soccer (futball) power, the party atmosphere of Rio de Janeiro, and the Amazon. We may also think of crime and poverty. What doesn't usually pop into our minds is the fact that Brazil is quickly emerging as a global economic power.

Given that Brazil has the world's sixth-largest economy and is growing quickly (it's neck and neck with France to be the world's fifth-largest economy), investors who are looking for long-term potential growth investments in international markets may want to take a hard look at the country. In addition, the upcoming World Cup and Olympics to be hosted by Brazil in the next five years may prove to be a catalyst for the market. In two instances, South Korea and China, an upcoming event of this magnitude proved to be the engine for stock market appreciation. What happens after the event is a different matter. Obviously what has happened in the past is not evidence of what will happen this time around, but it's something to keep an eye on.

Seth Zalkin, cofounder and managing partner at Astor Group, a global investment banking advisory firm that does a lot of work in Brazil, told me, "The World Cup and Olympics will bring significant economic and structural benefits to Brazil and will also advance the country's planning and infrastructure network. Increased investment in airports, the power grid, railways, roads and other transportation, hotels, telecommunications, and environmental projects will all have a long-term impact on the Brazilian economy that will transcend the direct impact of the actual events."[18]

The Brazilian story is about more than just gearing up for two major sporting events. As a country that is loaded with natural resources, Brazil is helping to feed the ravenous Chinese appetite for these resources. But when I add that it has a very young population and a growing middle class, I should have your attention. The Brazilian consumer has more disposable income than ever before and is spending it. It's an economy that is not just based on feeding China, as tourism is a key and growing economic driver.

The naysayers on Brazil point to the fact that if China goes bust, Brazil will go down with it. While I don't see that happening at all, there are ways to invest and gain exposure to sectors in the Brazilian economy that have little to do with China. Smaller Brazilian companies and companies that are exposed to the consumer are the way to go. This is an economy with an exploding middle class and with historically low unemployment, and no one can deny that people with jobs and a paycheck will spend money.

Figure 4.3 compares EWZ (at the bottom of the graph), which is the iShares MSCI Brazil Index, with two ETFs from the firm Global X. What you see is that the top performer, BRAQ (which is the Brazil consumer ETF), and the middle performer, BRAZ (which is the Brazil mid-cap ETF), have outperformed the EWZ. Thus, both the consumer sector and the mid-cap sector have outperformed the larger Brazilian companies as investments.

FIGURE 4.3 Brazil ETF Comparison

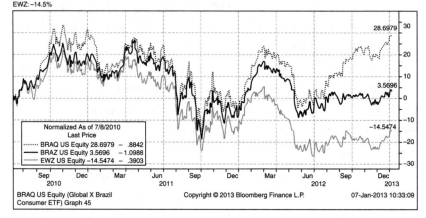

FIGURE 4.3 Brazil ETF Comparison

Will Brazil lead the rest of Latin America and become the emerging market of choice among investors? That's a tough question. Most institutional investors love Asia, as I have mentioned, and are not as quick to look at Brazil. On the other hand, Asia is very much about regional cooperation and geographic alliances in order to push forward. I think that's what many analysts are missing about the Brazil story. It's a huge country, and it has very quietly become an economic power. That is not something that will end any time soon.

Based solely on demographics, it is hard to imagine Brazil not becoming the third-largest economy in the world in a few decades. Germany and France just don't have the young populations needed to keep up strong growth. Brazil has everything and can become a country similar to the United States because it has sufficient natural resources to prevent it from having to rely on imports in order to survive. That even sets it apart from China, which relies on the world to feed it and provide goods for it. Since that isn't necessary in Brazil, I think that makes it the de facto emerging market leader.

Much like the ASEAN 10, the rest of Latin America and its frontier markets (especially Colombia, Peru, and Chile) is an area where you have a bunch of smaller countries setting the world on fire with incredible growth, very young populations, and solid, debt-free economies.

The stereotype of Latin America is that it's a place that is full of crime, corruption, and the constant threat of a military coup. That was then, and this is now. Believe it or not, most countries have begun cleaning up their acts, and while there is still crime, the situation is vastly improved. Most countries have become more open, and on the financial front, they have become models for how to run a country. Compared to most Western countries, which are bloated by huge amounts of debt and budget deficits, Latin American countries have been very conservative on the debt front. In fact, Chile is required by law to run a structural surplus. I have already mentioned so-called frontier markets like both Peru and Colombia, which are truly indicative of what's been going on south of the border.

Mario Felisberto told *Investment & Pensions Europe*, "What makes the region more attractive is that in the past 20 years, countries have gone through a lot of economic reforms, curbing inflation to make them more open to foreign direct investment." The chief investment officer of Latin America for HSBC Asset Management, Felisberto continued, "Many countries could now be considered true democracies. And demographic conditions there are generating huge potential in terms of consumption."[19]

In a world that is struggling to deal with funding older populations, is awash in debt, and in many cases is on the verge of bankruptcy, Latin America, and especially the frontier markets, deserves investment dollars.

Africa

A question that is frequently asked, both by clients and in the media, is where speculative investors should put their money. Investors want to know what's next. They realize that markets such as China can't keep moving up forever, so they want to find the "next" China and make a profit while they can.

Well, here is an idea that's not for the faint-hearted: Africa and the Middle East.

Africa usually conjures up images of hunger, drought, disease, and poverty. Think of the TV commercials featuring Sally Struthers asking for "just a few cents a day" to help keep a child out of poverty. Add to this political corruption and a seemingly endless list of coups and countercoups to seize power, and it doesn't sound like a particularly good prospect. The most positive visions that most people have of Africa are of the unusual species of animals that live there and the safaris that provide a wonderful view of nature. Most of us imagine an impoverished, backward continent that is relatively untouched by modern technology. Think of the classic movie from the early 1980s, *The Gods Must Be Crazy*. I'm not a movie reviewer, but here's the plot thumbnail: A group of bushmen find a bottle of Coke that has dropped from a passing airplane. They believe it's a gift from the gods, but in the course of the movie, they instead learn about personal property and what ensues when others want what you have.

Yet, despite the perceptions just mentioned, Africa is appearing more and more in the sights of many visionary investors.

Jason Voss, CFA, writes in Seeking Alpha, "Of Africa's 54 nations, only four are experiencing dangerous conflict. In fact, more than half of African nations have held democratic elections since 2006. Additionally, multi-party democracy continues to take hold across the continent."[20]

Africa is loaded with potential. With its abundance of natural resources, and after years of trying to figure out how to monetize these assets, strong economic growth has recently been seen throughout the region. But it's no longer just about natural resources. Voss quotes the CEO of the private equity firm Development Partners International, Runa Alam. He says, "Alam also highlighted that Africa is a continent growing by addressing its own internal economies and not just growing by exploiting its natural resources/commodities. In fact, she pointed out that Ethiopia is growing gross domestic product (GDP) at a rate of more than 15%, and yet, it has very little commodity wealth. Continent-wide, many entrepreneurs are specifically founding businesses to address the burgeoning middle class of Africa, which is estimated at 313 million people."[21]

Many Western countries that loaned the African nations billions of dollars have decided to give them debt relief, either by forgiving the entire debt or by creating very favorable repayment terms. This has given these upstart economies a clean slate and the opportunity to start off on the right foot. With this in mind, many companies dealing with the construction of basic infrastructure, including a number of Israeli concerns, have opened up shop in Africa.

I have a good friend, Gadi Weisberger, who used to share office space with me. He started growing paprika in Ethiopia. Why? Apparently there is a big global demand for paprika, and there just isn't enough of it. He told me on numerous occasions that while Ethiopia has come a long way, it has a very long way to go. He said that corruption was still the easiest way to get things done, and that there was lots of red tape.

In fact, many of the perceptions that we have of Africa, as mentioned earlier, are actually correct to a certain extent. For many of its inhabitants, clean water is still nonexistent, basic foodstuffs are limited, and there are no roads. Although international investment in Africa has picked up, it has been mostly focused on building the basic infrastructure in these countries. It is not a question of technological innovation that would rival that of Israel. Rather, this investment is involved in supplying the very basics to Africans, things that we all take for granted. They do know what Coca-Cola is!

In picking frontier markets for a retiree to invest in, I would stick to Peru and Chile and leave Africa for another day. Maybe your grandchildren should invest in Africa, but not you.

The Middle East

When you think of the Middle East, the first thing that comes to mind is oil, oil, and more oil. Sort of like the 1960s American comedy show *The Beverly Hillbillies* on steroids. For investors looking at investing in the region, there aren't all that many investment choices. It's difficult to gain exposure to the oil sector; the best way to do so is to buy the big multinational oil players. Most of the region's stock markets are quite small, not well developed, and illiquid. The two standouts are clearly Turkey and Israel. In these two countries, you have developed financial markets and well-diversified economies.

TURKEY

What's the hottest emerging market out there? Somewhere in Southeast Asia? Latin America? Nope, the answer is Turkey. Over the course of 2012, no major emerging market came close to replicating its huge gains.

For many people, Turkey remains an enigma, a country with a Western secular culture that is leaning toward Islam. Americans may not fully appreciate the role that the Turkish military plays in the overall culture of the country. It is paramount. Conventional wisdom says that as long as the Turkish military remains secular and committed to keeping Turkey secular, the country will continue to be stable and will partner well with the Western world. The problem is that the secularism of the military has become blurred. Many Islamists joined the military five years ago, and as they work their way up the ranks in the next five to eight years, they will play an important role in the military. This will threaten the military's longstanding secularism. If the military tilts toward the Islamist view of the world, it could push the country toward something resembling Egypt or Libya.

According to Natasha Gural of CNBC, "The Turkish economy rebounded from a severe crisis in 2000–2001 to emerge as the fastest-growing economy among the OECD countries and second fastest among G-20 countries, with a growth rate of 9 percent in 2010 and 8.5 percent in 2011. It is on track to become the leading OECD economy through 2017, with annual growth to average 6.7 percent."[22]

That is stunning growth in today's low-growth world. Coupling this with a strong banking system and a declining government debt burden, Fitch Ratings, back in November 2012, upgraded Turkey's sovereign debt to BBB-, the lowest rung on the investment-grade level. Again, in a world that is laden with debt and where many developed countries are having their debt downgraded, this is noteworthy.

Since it is a member of NATO, Turkey's security needs are also being taken care of. So what's not to like? Here are a few things: Regional unrest, domestic strife between secularists and Islamists, inter-ethnic battles and potential isolation. Turkey has used both the Arab Spring and the Syrian uprising as springboards to advance its influence in the region. The Turkish government believes that the country has the strongest economy and military in the area and will soon be the major player in the Middle East. However, its relations with the only democracy in the region, Israel, have been ice-cold for the last two and a half years. Its support for the rebels against Syria's Bashir Assad has alienated Turkish allies in Iran; the Syrian civil war is flooding Turkey with refugees; the Islamists have purged the former secular military; and as Sharia law is imposed on large segments of society, the economic contribution of women will decline drastically; it also looks like the European Union will never allow Turkish admission. Throw into the mix that Kurdish separatists are sensing an opportunity for independence, and we could see a Turkish version of the Arab Spring.

Even if Turkey achieves the regional dominance it seeks, Prime Minister Recep Tayyip Erdogan will face headwinds from all the aforementioned problems. Erdogan, who calls himself a "servant of Sharia" ushered in a new Islamist movement with a moderate-looking face. While many praise Turkey as a model for Muslim democracy, proponents appear to be glossing over some huge obstacles to even medium-term political and economic success and stability.

The test of his version of a Muslim democracy will come in the next few years. It's very difficult to impose secular values on a profoundly Muslim legacy; therefore Turkey can be a prime target for Islamists. If they get a foothold, we will see Turkey face a fate similar to that of many of the countries in the region, where leaders were swept away by the Arab Spring. This is not original thinking on my part. Dmitry Sedov wrote in the *Strategic Culture Foundation* that if the forecasted ascendency of Islamists in the military proves sound, "the series of crises will anything but leave Turkey unaffected."[23]

This potential risk, which could happen instantly, leaves me a bit hesitant about recommending Turkey as a must-invest country at this time.

ISRAEL

I mentioned Israel. As I live there, Israel is near and dear to my heart. But my living there doesn't make it a great investment.

While it is not a frontier market, Israel has become a hot investment destination for private equity firms and institutions like venture capital funds that are looking to invest in up-and-coming technology. In fact, rule number one in investing is not to become emotionally attached to an investment. So when speaking about Israel, I believe it's of utmost importance to differentiate between investing in the Israeli economy and investing in Israeli ingenuity.

While Israel has made it through the 2008 financial crisis without much damage, sporting 3 to 4 percent economic growth, a solid real estate market, and historically low unemployment, as I've said in this chapter, I can find 15 other countries with the same or better economic fundamentals. In fact, the local Tel Aviv Stock Exchange (TASE) has been underperforming major global indexes for more than two years.

When investors watched the military altercation with the terrorist group Hamas during the winter of 2012 and saw missiles launched by Hamas intercepted by the Iron Dome antimissile batteries, it was like a video game coming to life. They wanted a piece of this ingenuity and creativity. It's no secret that many of Israel's hottest technologies are consumer-based applications of military technology. Think back to the United States's space program and how our lives have been changed by the moon program technology. It's mind-blowing. As the global economy gains strength, and with increased IT spending by major corporations on the horizon, these companies have the potential to benefit.

Investors want to invest in companies that power the world. It's no secret that the largest multinational companies in the world are very active in Israel. From Microsoft to Johnson &

Johnson, IBM, and a multitude of other well-known companies, they come to Israel to acquire or invest in today's cutting-edge technologies. From companies that can put a camera in a pill to help alleviate the need for invasive gastro procedures (Given Imaging) to companies that lead the world in computer security (Checkpoint) to companies that are leading the move into cloud computing (Radware), what Israel does very well is power the world based on technology.

I could write a whole book on investing in Israel, but I will stop here. For those who are interested in investing in this space, feel free to shoot me an e-mail.

Canada

When it comes to investing, Canada rarely gets the headlines, but that may be a mistake. After all, Canada is not flashy, but it is consistent, and when it comes to investing, especially for retirement, slow and steady wins. Here's where I could quote facts and figures about the country's land mass, its relationship with the United States as its largest trading partner, and its being the top destination in the world for U.S. investment. What seems to interest more people is that Canada is the largest energy supplier to the United States (oil, natural gas, and electricity). Indeed, the country is loaded with natural resources, and while we have spoken about the Brazilian, Australian, and African model of selling commodities to feed the ravenous Chinese appetite, Canada does the same thing vis-à-vis the United States. Now Canada has also started to supply China with energy.

Being a leading natural resource supplier to both of the largest global economies is very impressive and bodes well for Canada's long-term economic prospects. Canadian banks have the reputation of being among the most conservative and safest in the world, and the country came through the financial crisis in good shape.

While everything sounds hunky-dory, there are some clouds looming on the horizon. A continued global economic slowdown will have a negative impact on both the price and the amount of sales of natural resources. And while the banks are solid, the Canadian consumer has learned a trick or two from his American cousins about debt. According to CBC News, "This spring, the average ratio of household debt to personal disposable income reached a record 163 per cent, up from 137 per cent five years earlier."[24] Not only will that affect the indebted consumer, but it will put more pressure on the banks.

Another trouble spot is a potentially overheated housing sector. The financial blogger the Dividend Guy writes on Seeking Alpha, "The simple fact that the CHMC has been reducing access to mortgages through several rule changes over the past three years is a clear example that the Canadian Government is concerned about the situation. At the moment, there are more condo towers being built in Toronto than there are on the U.S. east coast. Do you really feel that our economy is booming at this point?"[25]

Another ripple effect of a hot housing market would mean higher interest rates as a way of cooling it off. This would make the already very strong Canadian dollar even stronger, thus affecting exports adversely.

In short, I like Canada, but I would wait for more clarity regarding some potential economic issues before investing there.

Europe

Our last stop on our global tour is Europe. So much for my enthusiasm! Europe has many structural issues: a declining birthrate, loads of debt, aging populations, and stagnant economic growth. Sounds like a recipe for success, no?

Investors have been preoccupied with Greece, and to a lesser extent Spain and Italy, since 2010. Since then, I have written articles calling on Greece to follow the Argentinean model of 20 years ago and just declare bankruptcy. Reorganize, get a plan, and get out of the mess. Instead, we have more money loaned, more broken promises, and more bailouts, and we are in the same place. It's a money pit. Just cut your losses and move on.

This Greek risk has spilled over, and we see headlines on Spanish and Italian bailouts. Germany, which has a strong economy but went through some austerity to get its economy back on track a few years ago, is the one funding a lot of this. How long can that be sustainable? Either the concept of the euro will change or the currency will fall apart entirely. With this cloud overhead, it's hard to get too excited over Europe. That having been said, I mentioned earlier that investors need to keep their eyes open and not just sit back and do the buy and hold thing.

Tawhid Ali, director of research at AllianceBernstein European Value, is more optimistic. He writes, "Equity investors in Europe have long been waiting for something to spark a sustainable stock-market recovery. Today I think it's easier to see the catalysts for a potential rebound. The threat of a sovereign debt default has been alleviated by recent European Central Bank moves, along with the progress (albeit slow) made at various European Union summits in recent months. And with more than €1 trillion deployed to support bank liquidity, the euro-area banking system is also looking much more secure."[26]

He cites historically low valuations for most stocks. In many ways, I would agree. Many stocks have been subjected to the proverbial throwing the baby out with the bathwater. This means that regardless of a particular company's business prospects, investors have bailed out of Europe and dumped everything European, without discrimination. A stock that I have been showing my clients fits this example. Banco Santander is a Spanish bank that does more than 70 percent of its business outside the continent. Most of its business is done in Latin America. So even if Spain were to go under, it wouldn't hurt Banco Santander significantly. Throw in a dividend yield above 10 percent and you have one heck of an intriguing investment. This isn't a recommendation but it's idea generation and investors need to do their own research. In fact, for retirees, not only are European stocks cheap, but they are paying much higher dividends than their U.S. counterparts. For investors who are looking for income, this has the potential to be very interesting. I will get to the whole dividend story in the next two chapters, and, needless to say, it also favors investing internationally.

So while I don't have a lot of very long-term hope for Europe based on the dwindling middle class and low birthrate, for intermediate-term investors, there may be things to talk about.

SCANDINAVIA

Let's be honest. When you think of Sweden, Norway, Denmark, and Finland, what comes to mind? Female ski teams, freezing temperatures, long winters, and Olympic medals in events that involve several forms of sliding and jumping. But if you take a longer look at the region, you will find Europe's strongest economic fundamentals: a respectable growth rate (more than 3 percent), lower unemployment than in most of Europe, and tremendous fiscal discipline make this region the most intriguing investment on the continent.

If others look at Europe as an interesting investment destination because of its low value and high dividends, I would say that this may be a good idea for two years or so, but at some point the markets will catch up with the economic situation and cap the appreciation potential. What I like about Scandinavia is the long-term potential based on sustained growth.

Many advisors don't look at Scandinavia as a separate investment from the rest of Europe, but as you can see, I like to drill down a bit and break up geographies. I think that if you say "Asia," "Europe," or "Latin America" in general, you are not doing justice to the winners and losers in each geographic region. Since most investors lump Scandinavia with the rest of Europe, which is not on the radar screen right now for most investors other than the aforementioned contrarians, my advice is to take a long look at the region, but watch how it trades in relation to broader Europe.

I've summed up my view of how the world stacks up against the GPS retirement portfolio criteria in Appendix B, "Investment Criteria for International Markets." The criteria remain the same over time, so it's your job to assess how the countries align with these criteria when you're looking at them for your investment decisions.

After this whirlwind tour of the world, unpack your suitcases. Now we'll look at the instruments for investing in the best the world has to offer.

CHAPTER 5

Investing in Foreign Stocks

In my spare time, I dabble in matchmaking. Yes, that's right; I try to set people up so that they can get married. I have actually been successful three times. One thing I've learned about matchmaking with humans also applies to matching people with investments: we humans need to stop being superficial.

Here's what I mean. With the advent of online dating, singles tend to focus way too much on the exterior, that is, the looks of a prospective mate. Let's say you ask me if I know someone who might be a good match. As soon as I've suggested someone, and long before I can give my insights on why this person might be a great match, you've probably already Googled her name and been through all her Facebook pictures. People think they know so much about another person from such superficial information that they might even skip the first date. Ask any married person to tell you about the most attractive feature of his spouse, and you're going to hear more about the way she laughs or the way her eyes twinkle when she speaks to you than about whether she looks like a movie star.

Believe it or not, the same holds true for investments. It's especially true for stocks, mutual funds, and ETFs because, unlike the instruments we'll cover in Chapter 6, looks are more prone to deception with these. Even though an instrument has a certain mandate on how it's invested, you still have to look under the hood and make sure it really works for you; be sure you know what you're getting.

Investing in foreign stock markets can be quite different from what you're used to in the United States because their structures are different. Some markets are open for eight hours a day but allow retail investors to trade for only two of them, limiting the rest of the time to institutional investors. On its website, the Securities and Exchange Commission also advises investors about the risks that can come with different market operations across the globe. "Foreign markets often operate differently from the major U.S. trading markets. For example, there may be different periods for clearance and settlement of securities transactions. Some foreign markets may not report stock trades as quickly as U.S. markets. Rules providing for the safekeeping of shares held by custodian banks or depositories may not be as well developed in some foreign markets, with the risk that your shares may not be protected if the custodian has credit problems or fails."[1]

Other markets, like China's, may be closed to foreigners. As an example of how convoluted foreign markets can be, let's look at China. For those people who, despite my warning in Chapter 4, still feel the need to invest in Chinese stocks, the question is how to actually do it. The obvious answer would be, "buy stocks in China." Well, not so fast. If you want to invest in the United States, you buy U.S. stocks, and if you would rather buy stocks in Mexico, you buy Mexican stocks. But if you want to invest in Chinese stocks, there are four basic ways to do so.

First, you can buy the stocks of companies that are headquartered in China, but whose stocks trade in the United States. You can buy either ADRs (American Depository Receipts, mentioned in the next section) or anything else that is "Chinese listed." For U.S. investors, this is the easiest approach because you don't need to convert money into a foreign currency and you make the purchase in your own brokerage account.

The second option is the China "A" shares market. These are stocks that trade on the Shanghai and Shenzhen markets. Here you have Chinese companies trading in the local currency, the renminbi. This sounds like just what the doctor ordered. Well, that's fine, except that shares in the A shares market, are strictly off limits to non-Chinese investors.

The next option is the Chinese "B" shares market. The B shares are also shares of companies listed on the Shanghai and Shenzhen markets, except that they trade in U.S. dollars. Why do they trade in dollars? Because historically, this was a way to raise overseas capital. Sounds good. The problem is that the B market isn't very liquid.

Finally, we have the Hong Kong "H" shares. These are Chinese companies that trade in Hong Kong. They trade in Hong Kong dollars, which means that you will need to convert currency in order to buy them. For most investors, the best choice is to buy the Chinese companies that trade in the United States. Is your head spinning yet?

Let's discuss the three major vehicles for investing in foreign equities: common stocks, mutual funds, and exchange-traded funds (ETFs). When you are investing in foreign equities, keep in mind that while the vehicles are the same from country to country, the practicalities of investing in them are not as straightforward as buying U.S. stocks while living in Indianapolis. If you want to buy equities in the countries where they're issued, you may have to wade through a lot of rigamarole, some of which we'll cover here.

Be prepared for a lot of information on ETFs compared to the other topics in this chapter. They are a relatively new and cost-effective means for gaining international exposure, and because they've proliferated, investors shouldn't go into them blindly.

Finally, "international" can mean a lot of things. You've got to ask yourself, do you want broad-based exposure, or do you want to choose a region or make your decisions country by country?

Common Stocks

If you are a retiree and you have been saving and investing for many years, you already know what common stocks are. As a reminder, a common stock is a security that represents ownership in a corporation. Holders of common stock exercise control by electing a board of directors and voting on corporate policy. Stocks move up and down based on the company's projected fortunes and the movement of the overall market.

When it comes to foreign markets, there are two ways to purchase individual stocks: you can either buy them on a local exchange or buy an American Depository Receipt (ADR). ADRs are shares in foreign companies that are deposited in an institutional bank account in the United States. Receipts for the shares deposited are issued and traded on the U.S. exchanges. Those receipts represent the underlying shares held on deposit.

Since they are denominated in U.S. dollars, ADRs allow investors to buy shares in overseas companies without the costs associated with dealing directly in a foreign stock market. This means that the average small investor doesn't have to worry about the various currencies involved. Unfortunately, most companies don't have ADRs and choose to list their shares only in their home country.

DIVIDEND-PAYING STOCKS

In low-interest-rate environments, investors should take a long look at dividend-paying stocks as a way to help lower the market volatility of their portfolio and generate income. It's important to emphasize, however, that fixed-income investors who try to enhance the income generated from their portfolio solely through investing in dividend-paying stocks are doing so at their own peril. It's as if the proponents of dividend strategies are blind to the fact that investors can actually lose principal. If you are retiring with a couple of hundred thousand dollars, no matter how much income your dividends generate, you can't afford to see your net worth drop by 30 percent, which is entirely possible. These stocks are not a replacement for bonds, but nowadays, unfortunately, using them this way has become a popular approach.

Traditionally, yields on bonds outpaced the dividend yield on common stock. This is a reason that investors should incorporate bonds into their portfolio—to get a fixed yield and a reasonable level of safety. It wasn't long ago that you could get 5 to 8 percent on a good, safe bond and about 3 percent in dividends on a stock. That's not the case in 2013. If someone promises you a guaranteed 8 percent yield, you can be sure that there is something very fishy going on. Can you say Bernie Madoff? As interest rates have dropped to near zero, just lock up some money in a CD at your local bank and see what it gives you. This search for yield that has created an interesting situation, as in many cases, a company's stock dividend is much higher than the yield on the same company's bonds, meaning that investors can generate more income from the stock than they can get from the bond. Investors beware: no matter what its dividend, a stock is a stock, meaning that it can drop significantly.

Investors should know that international stocks pay higher dividends than their U.S. counterparts. This is very important for retirees who are looking for enhanced levels of income. Charles Lewis Sizemore, CFA, principal of Sizemore Capital and editor of the *Sizemore Investment Letter*, quoted some interesting statistics when we spoke in the autumn of 2012: The United Kingdom, France, and Germany all have yields over 3 percent, Italy weighs in at 4.5 percent, and Spain yields more than 5 percent. The differing measures for the United States that the *Financial Times* tracks range from 2.2 to 2.7 percent.[2]

THE INTERNATIONAL DIVIDEND ADVANTAGE: AN INTERVIEW WITH JEREMY SCHWARTZ, CFA, WISDOMTREE DIRECTOR OF RESEARCH

Q: Did you have to educate investors on the advantages of investing abroad?

Schwartz: There is a continuous education aspect. Most people are 75 to 80 percent invested in the United States because of the home country bias. If you go on a pure market cap basis, with no bets on any country, it should be 40 percent United States and 60 percent international. If you look at dividends, you will see that about $1 trillion in dividends was paid in 2012, but only $300 billion came from the United States and the rest was paid by foreign companies. When you look specifically at emerging markets, by our count, more than 90 percent of the market capitalization of emerging market equities is in dividend-paying stocks. A dividend-focused approach thus does not sacrifice significant representation of the emerging markets by eliminating constituents that do not pay dividends.

Q: Emerging market investing can be more volatile yet produce higher returns. How do you go about trying to manage risk?
Schwartz: There is no question that emerging markets are where the global growth is coming from. Historically, there is more volatility in returns in emerging markets. Where the S&P 500 may have a 15 percent long-term volatility, you will see 30 percent in emerging markets. That's why we are focused on dividend ETFs: because they are able to lower volatility. Our Emerging Markets Equity Income Index has 20 percent lower volatility over a five-year time period than the broader emerging market index. But there is no question but that you do get higher volatility in these markets, and investors need to know that.

Q: When investing globally, do you think investors should use individual stocks?
Schwartz: When you pick individual stocks or even specific countries, you end up taking on a lot of selection risk. It's a lot more diversified and less risky to invest in broad-based regional indexes. If you're comfortable that you have an information advantage on a particular stock, go for it, but if you don't think you have that information, why take the selection risk?

Q: According to conventional wisdom, active equity mutual fund managers have an edge over ETFs in less liquid markets, especially emerging economies, and they really provide added value. Should investors use mutual funds instead of ETFs in these markets?
Schwartz: Well I think it's a myth that active managers perform better in illiquid markets. We have research that shows that active managers have actually done better at providing added value in the United States than in international markets. The funds are more

expensive and have larger trading costs. Our emerging market dividend ETF has beaten 98 percent of all emerging market managers, so for most investors, ETFs would be the way to go.

Mutual Funds

Equity mutual funds are baskets of stocks managed by professional money managers whose job it is to make sure that you're not investing in a dud. The funds invest in accordance with their own mandate. For example, a mutual fund that invests in large-cap U.S. stocks has a "mandate" to invest in large companies in the United States. You won't find it investing in small stocks in Lebanon, since that's outside its mandate.

When we distinguish between *global* and *international* funds, it's not an exercise in semantics. There is a clear distinction. International funds generally limit their investments to companies based outside the United States, whereas global funds will have some U.S. exposure. If you are using a mutual fund for your non-U.S. exposure, the pure way to do so is with an international fund. If you use a global fund, you will have more U.S. exposure than you bargained for.

International mutual funds, as actively managed products, have teams of analysts on the ground who get good, timely information that can be used in making investment decisions. I do that kind of due diligence when I'm investing in Israeli companies. There's no comparison between sitting with a CEO in person and listening in on the quarterly conference call or reading a bland analyst's report. There is no substitute for sitting in the CEO's office, asking direct questions, and watching him squirm in his chair when an unpleasant issue arises. The average retiree doesn't plan to jet around the world finding the best stocks and won't have access to CEOs the way a mutual fund manager does.

A big advantage of mutual funds is that they give retail inves-tors the ability to own professionally managed, well-diversified portfolios of stocks and bonds, which would be nearly impossible for someone with a small amount of money to accomplish by buying individual stocks. The fund will handle currency conver-sions and pay any foreign taxes, and it is likely to understand the operations of the different foreign markets.

I've seen retirees benefit from the reinvestment feature of mutual funds: dividends earned can be channeled back into the fund to buy more shares. If you liked it enough to buy it, you like it enough to buy more of it.

As much as I appreciate professional management, the down-side of this advantage is that there can be a change in fund man-agers. Good managers tend to stick around, but pay attention if there is a change that you don't like. It may be time to shop for a new fund.

Oh, and lest you think that all this professionalism is free, think again. The 12b-1 fees, partly paid out to the broker, can have a severe impact on performance, especially over the long term.

Finally, when you are considering mutual funds, consider the impact of capital gains that you might be liable for, even if they were generated before you bought in. You might be paying for someone else's gains, even if you are actually sitting on a loss. How does this work? Let's say that you buy Fund X on May 23, 2013. Let's say that over the first 4½ months of 2013, the fund manager had eliminated her position in Apple, which had been one of the fund's holdings. Keep in mind that she bought it back in 2009, so she was sitting on gains of hundreds and hundreds of percent. By the time you bought the fund in May, it no lon-ger owned Apple, but you are going to get stuck with a huge capital gains distribution because of the huge profit she made on the stock.

THE PATRIOT ACT AND YOUR FOREIGN RESIDENCY

I must highlight that for U.S. citizens who live abroad, mutual funds have become much trickier investments. Thanks to compliance requirements resulting from the Patriot Act, many firms require a U.S. address on an account. Without one, they will not allow a U.S. citizen to do business with them. They will even cancel the accounts of longstanding clients who have moved out of the country. This trend has been gaining in momentum, even among the largest and best-known fund families.

As an advisor based in Israel with both U.S. and Israeli securities licenses and a global clientele, I can't tell you how often I receive phone calls from investors who are being tossed out of firms that they have been with for decades. Thankfully, I have years of experience dealing with these issues and am able to find beneficial solutions for clients. If you are or may be in this situation, speak with an advisor who is set up and equipped to deal with these accounts, or else you will be severely limited in your investment options. For more on this topic, consult Chapter 7.

Exchange-Traded Funds

Exchange-traded funds (ETFs) are securities that track a stock or bond index and allow the investor to track that specific index closely by buying this one particular product. For example, if an investor wants exposure to the S&P 500 stock index, he can either buy all 500 stocks, which would be very costly and time-consuming, or he can purchase an ETF that will track the S&P index nearly point for point.

Because of their low costs and their simplicity, ETFs have become the fastest-growing financial tool used by investors. The financial media are full of advice for individual investors on how to use ETFs to create well-diversified investment portfolios. As part of their drive to convert investors to do-it-yourself (DIY) investing, they preach that you can have a great portfolio using low-cost ETFs. Despite all the attention that ETFs get and their surging popularity, however, many investors don't really understand what they are and how they are to be used. Not only that, but there are thousands of ETFs out there, so how is an investor to choose?

Since this is a fairly new product compared to mutual funds and stocks, not all advisors use them, and many retirees don't know how they might benefit from using them. I'll remedy that here.

Compared to individual stocks, by definition ETFs provide investors with a well-diversified global portfolio through exposure to hundreds, if not thousands, of different stocks. As a bonus, the ETF does this without requiring an investor or advisor to watch and follow a myriad of securities.

Another benefit of investing in ETFs is liquidity. Because they trade like individual stocks, ETFs can be bought and sold throughout the trading day, thus allowing active traders to try to time the market and cash in on intraday market moves.

Your cost basis is calculated from your purchase price, and since ETFs are mostly passive, meaning that they are not actively traded except for updating the index, there is little in the way of capital gains tax.

Finally, ETFs are very cheap. For the most part, they are passive instruments; therefore, they don't have the high fees that are associated with more actively managed vehicles.

The higher fees associated with mutual funds that charge up-front loads may encourage investors to hold them longer, thus enhancing their performance. But because ETFs can be traded from minute to minute, they have turned into a speculators' tool. For investors who want to create a portfolio using ETFs, the temptation to buy and sell is always there because of the low costs. Even retirees can get sucked in to trying to time the market.

Most ETFs are mirrors of indexes, making them passive investments. When you are dealing with foreign stock market indexes or even specific countries on an index, you have to take the good with the bad. Unfortunately, there is some bad. Here's an example: If your index is composed of 100 stocks, chances are that the bottom 50 probably aren't all that attractive on their own. What would be a micro-cap stock in the United States might be a large-cap stock in Thailand, but because the index is required to have 100 stocks, these companies fit the bill. That's a definite downside. Compare this to actively managed mutual funds, discussed previously.

Some ETFs don't always live up to investors' expectations. This is not the fault of the ETF; rather, it's the fault of the investor who's trying to manage her own portfolio. Folks, these instruments can be complex. You might think that your ETF gives you exposure to all of, say, Colombia, when in reality, only two or three Colombian stocks make up 70 percent of the entire ETF. This isn't necessarily bad, but it's not the diversified Colombian portfolio you told yourself you were buying. Either take the time to perform due diligence on your choices or pay an expert to do it for you.

HOW TO CHOOSE ETFs

There are several ETFs in any given asset class. Take, for example, small-cap stocks that trade in the United States. There are tens of products for this asset class, and while they may all appear to do the same thing, each has different criteria for tracking its chosen underlying indexes. This is why most DIY investors don't know about the striking differences between one ETF and the next.

Here's a cautionary tale for the DIY investor. In late 2012, the Vanguard Emerging Markets ETF changed its benchmark index. It stopped tracking the MSCI Emerging Markets index and started tracking an FTSE Emerging Market index. Why? To keep its fees lower. In order to use an index to make an ETF, the issuer must pay a licensing fee to the index, and this causes issuers to shop for price among the indexes.

If you don't know why this is a big deal, that's a reason to reconsider a DIY approach. The FTSE index doesn't include South Korea, which is a substantial player in emerging markets. So if you own the Vanguard Emerging Markets ETF, you no longer have exposure to South Korea. In my view, South Korea is still an emerging market (not a developed market, as FTSE classifies it). South Korea's performance over the last 10 years has boosted the performance of the MSCI Emerging Market index. The upshot: two emerging market ETFs are two different products. This is why you shouldn't go it entirely alone.

Traditionally, the index of choice for small-cap stocks is the Russell 2000. Russell compiles the index by ranking (in order of market capitalization) its total U.S. equity universe, which consists of up to 4,000 companies. The ETF issuer also takes into account the market value of the company and the level of the stock price when compiling the index.

Of course there are other small-cap indexes, like the S&P SmallCap 600. To gain admission into this index, stocks must show positive earnings growth for four successive quarters, which means that this index tracks growing companies that are making money.

What makes the difference in indexes even more important are the returns. According to data provided by WisdomTree,[3] over the last 15 years, the S&P SmallCap index has outperformed the Russell 2000 by 1.8 percent per year, with less risk. For investors, it doesn't get better than that: higher returns and lower risk. Most DIY investors would never know such statistics, and they can end up leaving lots of money on the table as a result. The differences in which index they choose and how they link to the index is more important than the expense comparison found in DIY platforms. Sometimes you get what you pay for.

The financial media encourage investors to use index funds and ETFs as a way to save money while having perfect portfolios. They don't mention that you might do your portfolio damage by not understanding the underlying mechanics of a particular ETF, by not staying vigilant on the changes in how the ETF follows an index, and by not keeping up with new ETFs that are constantly hitting the market.

CORE ETF PORTFOLIOS

How can an investor capture the advantages of ETFs (low cost and well diversified) without having to wade through the thousands of products that are available? More and more financial advisors have begun offering professionally managed "core ETF" portfolios through their firms. These portfolios are globally diversified using basic ETFs. They follow mathematical models that help the investor obtain a well-diversified portfolio, while limiting some of the volatility that comes with investing. Professional management creates the benefit of being linked to many stock indexes and knowing that the most appropriate ETFs are being used. This strategy has created strong competition with the mutual fund business, which was built on active management, but the underlying ETFs make the portfolio cheaper than a mutual fund. Managers of core ETF portfolios are actively managing a low-cost portfolio of passive investments, and this provides investors with the best of both worlds: an actively managed portfolio and low costs.

Beware when you look at their results, however, because past performance does not guarantee future returns. It may be worthwhile to ask your investment advisor if ETFs can be used to diversify your portfolio in a low-cost, efficient manner. Unfortunately, I know financial advisors who offer professionally managed ETF portfolios and charge a 2 to 2.5 percent management fee. What chutzpah; after all, the whole point is to have a *low-cost* investment.

I've chosen to use interviews with managers from Global X and WisdomTree because these players have come into the ETF market focused on international markets with interesting methodologies and solutions to problems with the traditional ETFs. I am not a paid or reciprocated advocate for any of them, and I personally use a great many products from a long list of issuers on behalf of my clients.

With that said, none of these products is patented, and other issuers could come into the market with enlightened thinking and approaches similar to those I've introduced to you here. As ETFs proliferate, they have become more specialized, with a host of new strategy ETFs coming to market. Some of these may even employ active strategies, which is truly an evolution of the passive ETFs that investors were getting used to. This is good for investing, but difficult for investors, who face a daunting due-diligence task before buying them for their own portfolios.

INTERVIEW WITH BRUNO DEL AMA, CEO AND PORTFOLIO MANAGER OF GLOBAL X FUNDS

Q: What has made you focus on spaces (countries) that "traditional" ETF providers neglected?

del Ama: As a company, we can't really add much value by creating "me-too" products or another S&P 500 ETF, so we often seek out areas where we see significant growth potential that other ETF providers may have overlooked. At Global X, we believe that the primary way we can add value for investors is by creating products that provide access to areas of the market where we see significant growth opportunities, and where the current investment options may be limited. Our first ETF, the Global X FTSE Colombia 20 ETF (GXG), is a great example of this belief, as Colombia was a country where we saw a tremendous growth opportunity, but where many other providers saw a higher-risk country with a history of security issues. We believed that the security situation and political environment in Colombia had already materially improved and were significantly better than investors perceived. It is therefore not a surprise that Colombia has been one of the best-performing markets in the world since we launched this ETF. At the time we launched the product, there really was no easy, cost-efficient way to invest directly in Colombia. There were a couple of ADRs that traded on the New York Stock Exchange, but the options were limited. Even if you were a hedge fund or an institutional investor, the cost of operating directly in Colombia was fairly prohibitive. The combination of the growth opportunity and lack of investment options for Colombia created, in our opinion, the perfect environment to create an ETF that would track the local market.

Q: Another such product is your SuperDividend ETF (SDIV), which is truly globally diversified. In a world where investors are desperate for yield, there is nothing like it. What was behind the reason to launch it?

del Ama: SDIV was inspired by a very successful hedge fund manager. By his own account, a large part of this manager's success was due to what he described as an entire market segment that was overlooked by most investors—"super-dividend" (approximately 8 to 15 percent) equity securities. Investors often perceived these high-yielding companies as higher risk, but the historical data did not justify this perception. While this yield/risk relationship holds true in the fixed-income space, where higher yield is achieved only by taking additional risk (lower credit quality, higher duration, and so on), historical analysis shows that as a group, super-dividend equities have outperformed lower-yielding equity groups by a significant margin over the last 10 years. Even more counterintuitive was the fact that the volatility of super-dividend equities was not higher than that of the other groups in many of the time periods, which implied that investors' perception of this entire space was not supported by the historical data. Of course, when designing the fund itself, we recognized that both country and company-specific risk were important diversification concerns, and this is what prompted the idea of making SDIV a global fund and equally weighting all of the 100 components.

Q: A knock on some international ETFs is that they don't really give you full exposure to the local market you are trying to invest in—that is, two or three stocks may end up having 60 to 70 percent of the ETF's weighting. What do you think about that?

del Ama: At Global X, we have actually addressed this issue directly with one of our Brazil funds, the Global X Brazil Mid Cap ETF (BRAZ). We noticed that in this market, the largest funds focused on Brazil are dominated by a few multinational companies—Petrobras and Vale alone account for about 30 percent of the fund exposure. While these are indeed Brazilian companies, the reality is that they are increasingly tied to the global economy (and the energy and materials markets) rather than to domestic Brazil. By focusing on the mid-caps, BRAZ offers much different exposure and a more targeted play on the local economy. With BRAZ, investors get more access to local companies that are more dependent on the growth that's happening on the ground in Brazil rather than on the growth of the global economy. Ultimately, the right ETF choice really depends on the investor's desired exposure and how he can best express his investment idea.

What's the Perfect Blend of Stocks, Mutual Funds, and ETFs?

Did you ever go shopping for a new car? Should you buy the cheapest car? The car with the best gas mileage? You can ask a never-ending series of questions, but at some point, you must make a decision. Figuring out which assets to use is a similar process. You need to use the products that will help you achieve your goals in the best fashion. You may even use multiple vehicles, like the family that owns both a minivan and a Mini Cooper. Investors need to do what's best for them, and not be a slave to conventional wisdom.

Determining whether to use an individual stock or a specific mutual fund or ETF has a lot to do with the size of an investor's portfolio. For smaller portfolios, picking and following individual stocks may be fun, but it's impractical. While I am not the greatest fan of a bland, generic diversification—as I mentioned in previous chapters—there is a need for some amount of diversification. A small account (anything under $150,000) using individual securities is going to be hard-pressed to achieve that, which is why mutual funds, ETFs, or both make more sense than individual stocks for such accounts.

In a low-interest-rate world where retirees need to generate more cash flow to meet their expenses, dividend yields on foreign stocks are significantly higher than those on their U.S. counterparts.

HOW MANY STOCKS IS "ENOUGH"?

Money magazine columnist Jason Zweig[4] wrote that investors who had a more concentrated portfolio (that is, who owned a smaller number of stocks) actually showed better returns than those who owned a lot of stocks. Roughly 8 percent of the top performers had their portfolios concentrated in a single stock.

Wow, that sounds very encouraging—until you read the rest of the findings, which reveal that among those with a concentrated portfolio, a lucky few hold stocks that can generate returns to the tune of hundreds of percent (we call these "super stock portfolios"). These make the group's average return look great, although the vast majority of the individual members of the group in fact show very poor results. Their stocks dropped sharply. This goes to show that you need to get behind the headlines.

I've seen both sides of this phenomenon. Back during the tech bubble of the late 1990s, I had a client who told me that he was going to put all his money into Nokia stock so that in a decade he would become a multimillionaire. He did just that, and things were going swimmingly until the tech bubble burst. Nokia has been in a downward spiral ever since. Needless to say, he won't be endowing any university department chairs in the foreseeable future.

Putting this into perspective, for every little old lady who made millions in Coca-Cola stock, there are many more investors who lost substantial amounts of money trying to hit a home run.

Even stocks that seem safe can turn into a danger zone. If we turned back the clock 20 years and asked investors for 20 safe stocks, at least a handful of the companies named will have gone bankrupt, be on the verge of bankruptcy, or have seen their share prices decimated. Sprint, Kodak, General Electric, Lehman Brothers, and Fannie Mae are just a few of the names that come to mind. The question many investors face is how many stocks they should own in order to be well diversified and to have the individual securities add to their account value. Remember the little old lady who bought a few shares of Coca-Cola 60 years ago and now donates millions and millions of dollars to the state university. She put all her eggs in one basket, and it worked out.

But is this the right strategy for you? Let's just say "your mileage may vary."

Professional money manager Roger Nusbaum of Your Source Financial says that individual stocks should represent no more than 2 to 3 percent of an overall portfolio[5] because if you own only 10 stocks with nothing else to diversify them, and one of them blows up, you're sunk. Most investors can't keep track of 50 stocks. If you hold 25 to 30 stocks, you can probably follow each company while enjoying enough diversity to lower your portfolio's volatility. My own personal preference for individual stocks is in the 25 to 30 range, simply because people aren't computers.

INTERVIEW WITH CHARLES LEWIS SIZEMORE, CFA, PRINCIPAL OF SIZEMORE CAPITAL AND EDITOR OF THE *SIZEMORE INVESTMENT LETTER*

Q: What is your approach to investing?

Sizemore: I generally take a contrarian value approach with a strong emphasis on dividend income. An ideal investment for me would be an American or European multinational with large exposure to emerging markets and a long history of rising dividends. I also tend to favor stable, predictable companies with a consumer focus.

Q: When investing internationally, do you think investors should invest more broadly or drill down to specific countries or regions?

Sizemore: This is going to depend on the investor's personality, investment style, and risk tolerance. To the extent that the investor's disposition allows it, I recommend drilling down to as specific a market as possible. If you've done your homework and you have reason to believe that, say, Turkish mobile phone providers or Brazilian beer brewers are underpriced, then why not invest directly in the companies that are most affected?

Q: What are your favorite markets?

Sizemore: This is something that changes as market conditions change, but right now I see a lot of value in European blue chips. European stocks are cheap right now because investors worry about growth in the Eurozone and because of the perceived risk that the entire European political project could come unwound. But European companies also tend to have the best indirect exposure to emerging markets, and they tend to pay reasonably high dividends. If you are willing to tolerate some amount of current volatility, Europe is fertile ground for long-term value.

Q: Why do you think investors should use a professional money manager as opposed to doing it themselves, using index funds and ETFs to invest globally?

Sizemore: It's a matter of expertise. You don't do your own medical treatment or build your own house; why should you treat your finances any differently? That said, good help can be hard to find. And you have to keep an eye on your money manager to make sure you are comfortable with the risk that she is taking. Some investors might very well be equipped to do their own investing (and, for that matter, serve as their own doctor). But it's always a good idea to get a second opinion.

ETFs AND MUTUAL FUNDS

I find that ETFs and mutual funds often complement each other, and therefore I like to use them both. While I love ETFs, they are not the aspirin of investing. There are certain niches where there are no ETFs or, if there are one or two, they are very thinly traded and may be on the verge of shutting. Take, for example, floating-rate and senior bank loan funds in the United States. There is basically just one ETF that tracks this space, but there are numerous mutual funds. The ETF for this space is very small and hasn't gained a lot of traction. Also, in country ETFs two or three stocks can often make up 70 to 80 percent of the whole ETF.

Country-specific mutual funds are more diverse. With an ETF, you aren't really investing in a specific country; rather, you're investing in the large electric and phone companies, which is probably not what you set out to do. Jeremy Schwartz, head of research at WisdomTree, a large ETF provider, told me that WisdomTree specifically creates its global ETFs to avoid this problem. No country has more than a 10 percent weighting. Problem solved!

Figure 5.1 gives you a quick way to compare ETFs and mutual funds.

BROAD INDEX, REGIONAL, OR COUNTRY-SPECIFIC?

Let's address this first for indexes and ETFs, then for mutual funds. This brings us to the question of whether to invest internationally through a very broad global index or by focusing on a region or on specific countries. DIY investors may choose to go the route of a broad-based international approach, because without political and economic expertise in countries or regions throughout the world, they could choose poorly. Going with a broad global index might sound attractive at first blush, but you have to look beyond the name of the index fund. For example, one of the most tracked indexes is the MSCI All Country World index. "All Country World index" sounds pretty good. The problem with this particular index, at the time of this writing, is that it allocates about 42 percent of its holdings to the United States and only 2 percent each to emerging economies like China and Brazil, whereas based on gross domestic product, China is the second-largest global economy. If you are trying to diversify your

FIGURE 5.1   ETFs and Mutual Funds: A Comparison

	ETFs	Mutual Funds
Fund expense	Low	Varies
Holdings transparency	Yes-daily	Yes, but delayed
Investment style	Usually passive	Generally active
Redemption fees	None	Sometimes
Brokerage fees	Yes	No; may have up-front or back-end load

portfolio to the rest of the world and you end up gaining U.S. exposure, your mission is far from accomplished.

That leaves the regional or country-specific approach, which I prefer. Why would I want large-scale exposure in Western Europe when I believe the future of economic growth in the world will come from Asia and Latin America? Think of my preference as being like approaching a spiked fruit punch: if the lemonade and vodka are the essentials you want, why dilute it with pineapple juice?

There is a big difference between investing in a broad-based international mutual fund and investing in regional funds. Since mutual funds are actively managed, if you are going to invest in a global fund, you need a manager who is an expert on the entire world. Even I don't pretend to be that smart, although I am close. By going regional, you get managers who specialize in smaller geographic regions, and that's where they are able to add value. I look at broad international funds as a marketing tool; the funds tell investors to go global, and they do that, but it's a watered-down version of going global. These are firms with large staffs of analysts who are getting paid to give their two cents. Why don't the firms put their money where their mouth is, pick winning markets, and filter out the losers?

How to Formulate Your Portfolio

Getting back to our original question of which vehicles to use, when it comes to larger accounts, I like to use all three vehicles: ETFs, mutual funds, and individual stocks. I think that there is a place for individual stocks as a way to either enhance income by focusing on higher-dividend stocks, identify specific opportunities, or both. I used the example of Banco Santander in the previous chapter. There you have a specific opportunity (a beaten-up stock that investors might not be rationally evaluating, throwing off a hefty dividend of more than 10 percent). You will not be able to achieve dividend levels of 10 percent in the current market environment with either ETFs or mutual funds.

It's hard enough to keep track of your grandchildren's birthdays, let alone trying to follow the comings and goings of 25 to 30 companies. That's why I encourage investors to use mutual funds and ETFs and leave 10 to 15 percent of their portfolio available for individual stocks on an opportunistic basis.

Many times I will add individual stocks to a portfolio that is mostly made up of ETFs and mutual funds. There may be a dividend opportunity, some kind of crisis where a particular stock has gotten slaughtered unjustly, or even a particular market where I may have knowledge. When these opportunities come along, I add them. For example, I have expertise in Israel. I often meet with the CEOs and CFOs of small, publicly traded Israeli companies that trade in the United States on the Nasdaq. In many cases, by global standards, these are small companies that are not on too many analysts' radar screens. I am able to get good information from these senior executives, information that's publicly available, but since no one is watching the stock, I am able to take advantage of this, buy for my clients, and then let the growth scenario play out.

How can the average retiree follow this strategy? If you don't want to call me, focus on what you know. Perhaps you might follow an industry that you retired from and look for stocks that have been unjustly hurt.

Caution: Hot Money

Beware of investing in markets that have high levels of "hot money," no matter which instruments you hold. First, let's try to understand what hot money is. Hot money refers to the flow of funds, or capital, from one country to another or from one sector to another in order to make a short-term profit. The danger is that these inflows and outflows can cause a lot of economic instability in the local markets and have even led to major global economic crises. In lay terms, hot money is a lot of money chasing a small amount of goods, or investments, which drives up the price at first, only to have them plummet as soon as people move their money somewhere else.

Recall the 1997 Asian financial crisis. There was a lot of foreign currency chasing after returns in Thailand and South Korea, to name two countries. When the music stopped, investors pulled out immediately, sending the local currencies into free fall.

Leading up to the year 2000, investors bought any stock on the tech-heavy Nasdaq. Investors couldn't care less what the company did, as long as it involved technology. All was good through March 10, 2000. I have perfect recall of that date because I married my wife two days later. The market may have started a 2½-year crash in March, but I started a life of marital bliss that has only gotten better and better. I figure that if my wife, who isn't too interested in investing, makes it this far into the book, she gets the reward of seeing my take on the "state of our union" in print.

In 2013, smaller and illiquid markets like Thailand and Vietnam are worth keeping an eye on. If they are indeed seeing hot money, when professionals bail en masse, it's usually Joe Retail Investor who gets left holding the bag. On the bright side, in many global markets, especially Brazil and a good chunk of Asia, that have been struggling over the last couple of years, the risk of a hot money crisis is unlikely.

For those whose stock portfolio took a beating, it's tempting to try to make up for that loss by doubling down or investing in a hot money market. As a frustrated blackjack player, I can attest that doubling down rarely works. If you're a retiree who suffered losses, keep your gunpowder dry. There are more conservative ways to recover than buying risky stocks. You need to understand the power of international bonds before making a final asset allocation decision. And with that, let's go to Chapter 6.

CHAPTER 6

How to Invest in Foreign Bonds

Once, at my nine-year-old son's Little League game, a father on the other team came over to get some free advice on his portfolio. All I wanted to do was watch my son play first base while keeping my three-year-old from taking a sand bath in the sandbox beside the bleachers, but what can I say? Requests for free advice are an occupational hazard. This father, who was not a client of mine either then or now, decided that obtaining some free financial advice was a better use of his time than watching eight- and nine-years-olds playing like the Bad News Bears, so he proceeded to tell me his life story.

A few baseball errors later, he finally got to the point. He was in his late forties, had made some good money when the high-tech company he worked at was sold, and was contemplating early retirement. He said he was trying to figure out how he could create a stable income stream and avoid taking much risk, so I suggested that he should incorporate bonds into his port- folio. He said, "What, are you crazy? Who wants to make 2 to 4 percent annually? I am looking at trying to get 9 to 10 percent annually." I reminded him that he had just said that he wanted a stable income stream and low risk, and in today's environment, he wouldn't get anywhere near 10 percent a year without having almost all his money invested in stocks, which means risk.

He actually started arguing with me, the dispenser of free advice, so I said that I had actually come to watch my son, not to get into an argument over his portfolio. Needless to say, I have never heard back from him, although I can't wait to see what happens when we play them next season!

I don't tell that story just to illustrate how high-strung people can get about their investments. I tell it because it's just not computer programmers who misunderstand bonds; even some professional investors have no concept of how bonds work. Here's proof. I have a client with a large portfolio who happens to live in a community with a few retired mutual fund managers from a very, very well-known mutual fund family. He gets advice from them (I reckon that it's free as well; notice a pattern!) on what he should do with his portfolio. He takes a very pessimistic view of the world and believes that World War III is just around the corner. As a result, he is very risk-averse. In 2010, I suggested that he move a significant amount of money into various bonds. He asked his so-called advisors, and they told him, "No way. Keep your money in stocks and just wait it out; even if things go south, they will go back up in the future." Well, that's easy for them to say because they are worth more than $20 million each. But for my client with $2 million, a 20 to 30 percent market drop would have a severe impact on his retirement.

After some back and forth, it turned out that the so-called advisors admitted to my client that they had no concept of how bonds even work, and that they knew only stocks. I guess the moral of all this is that you get what you pay for!

Why are bonds so misunderstood? Because investors have been force-fed by the financial media with the belief that owning stocks is the secret to financial success. Even if you are retired, just hold onto your stocks and all will be well. So let's talk about bonds and alternative investments like real estate, private equity, and foreign currencies. After all, there's more to an investment portfolio than just stocks.

Understanding Bonds

Let's take a minute and explain what bonds are. A bond is essentially a loan or an IOU issued by a corporation, government, or government agency. When a person buys a bond, she is basically loaning money to the issuer. In return, the bondholder expects to receive her money back when the bond matures (the agreed-upon date for the issuer to repay the principal), as well as receiving interest payments, which are usually paid semiannually.

What about so-called junk bonds? They work the same way as traditional corporate bonds, but the rating agencies give them lower ratings because they're more speculative. Bonds rated below investment grade, or "BBB–" because of their higher potential default risk, are referred to as junk. I am not a huge fan of the term. The fact is that the default rate on most junk bonds is not substantially higher than that on investment-grade bonds, but they have a much higher yield.

The term *junk bond* conjures up all kinds of bad memories as we go back in time to the 1990 scandal involving Michael Milken. Milken developed the junk bond market. He saw that bonds that paid much higher yields weren't as risky as many people thought, so he used junk bonds to help companies raise cash. Many companies with emerging technologies were able to fund their businesses by using these bonds. Cellphone pioneer Craig McCaw, MCI Communications, media mogul Ted Turner, and other cable companies and hotel companies owe their businesses, and we owe our technological progress, to Milken.

What brought him down was the teaming up of large corporations and the U.S. government, which is a case of strange bedfellows, for sure. Those were the days of corporate raiders, who would try to buy large companies that weren't being run efficiently through what were called leveraged buyouts (LBOs). Milken's firm, Drexel Burnham, would provide the raiders with a letter confirming that it would stand behind the raiders and give them the necessary financing to complete the corporate takeover. The raiders would take an equity position in the target company, and even if the raid was unsuccessful, they would profit handsomely, as the price of the target's stock would surge based on the takeover rumors. His part in this obviously made Milken a target.

In 1989 he was indicted and the firm's assets were frozen, using the Racketeer Influenced and Corrupt Organizations Act of 1970 (RICO). This was the first time an individual who had no ties to organized crime had been prosecuted under the Act. When they went after his brother Lowell, Milken had no choice but to agree to a plea bargain. Did he commit securities violations? Possibly. But what he did with the junk bonds was completely legal. Many people, myself included, believe that the unprecedented economic boom from the mid-1980s through the 1990s was a direct result of his providing capital to upstart companies.

HOW DO BONDS WORK?

Let's say Microsoft issues a bond that matures in four years and has a fixed interest rate of 3 percent with payments made semiannually. If a person invests $10,000 in this bond, he will receive

$150 every six months, or $300 annually. Four years from now, Microsoft will repay the investor the original $10,000 as well.

Note that the guarantee to pay interest and principal at maturity comes from the issuer of the bond. In this example, if Microsoft were unable to meet its obligations, the bond would default, and the bondholders would lose some or all of their money, as they would not receive the remaining interest and the principal.

Bonds are liquid investments, which means that the bondholder does not have to hold on to them until they mature, but can sell them whenever she wants, at which point she receives the interest that has accrued to that point. However, there is no guarantee of principal at this time; the bond will be sold at the market price, which may be higher or lower than the initial purchase price. I am not going to discuss municipal bonds here, because most countries don't have them, and the tax advantages for U.S. citizens go beyond the focus of this book. For retirees, munis can play an important role in their fixed-income portfolio, so consult with a qualified advisor.

BOND PRICES

Two main issues affect the prices of bonds. They move in response to changes in the credit quality and financial situation of the issuer, and to shifts in interest rates. With corporate bonds, changes in the company's financials can both positively and negatively affect the price. Changes in interest rates usually have the most impact on bond prices. Here's how. Bear with me, as this is a bit complicated.

There is an inverse relationship between changes in interest rates and bond prices. When interest rates decline, the prices of existing bonds usually rise, and when interest rates climb, prices usually fall. The reason for this can be explained using the example of the 3 percent Microsoft bond given earlier. If interest rates fall, the 3 percent received on this bond becomes more attractive, and as the demand for the bond increases, so does the price. Conversely, if interest rates move up, suddenly the 3 percent isn't as attractive as it was when rates were lower, so the price of the bond drops.

For most investors who have used bonds, their familiarity with bond markets usually ends with the United States, which means that they've heard of government and high-quality corporate bonds, and, to a much lesser degree, high-yield bonds.

When it comes to investing in bonds issued outside of the United States, most retirees don't know why they should bother investing in foreign bonds, what instruments are available, and how to access them. I believe a main reason for this is that in some respects, Americans are spoiled. The U.S. dollar enjoys reserve currency status, so the closest they get to foreign currency is playing Monopoly. Maybe that's harsh, but Americans are provincial when it comes to foreign currency, which makes it easy to understand why they think that all their money should be in dollars.

There aren't many other countries where investors would feel comfortable keeping all their money locked into one currency. Outside of the United States, investors hold multiple currencies. Go to Australia, Canada, or the United Kingdom, and you will see wealthy investors diversifying their holdings into multiple currencies. In addition to travelers, who need the local currency to conduct their affairs, other retirees who want to hold foreign currencies should do so by holding bonds that are denominated in foreign currencies. My approach is to buy bonds denominated in currencies that I think have mid- to long-term staying power. The bond gives you enhanced income over putting your money into a local deposit in that currency. You get a better yield this way.

I don't see value in a retiree holding $150,000 in Australian dollars and staring at his computer screen waiting for a 1.5 percent uptick so that he can cash out and convert it back to U.S. dollars in order to fund his retirement. By focusing on currencies with fundamentals at their backs, then finding appropriate bonds in those currencies, retirees get both a diversified portfolio and enhanced income. I'm not advocating that retirees become sophisticated currency traders. Foreign exchange, while the world's largest market, is also one of the most volatile. In order to profit, you need to always have your finger on the trigger, and if you aren't able to react fast enough, you lose. If you want to spend your retirement staring at a computer screen, then go for it. If you are like 99 percent of retirees, leave foreign exchange (forex) trading for the professionals.

WHO NEEDS THEM?

The most frequent question that I get from investors is, "I live in the States; what point is there in my owning foreign bonds? Aren't they a lot more risky?" The reason to own them is twofold: increased returns and higher income along with lower risk. These combine to form the holy grail of investing.

According to Douglas J. Peebles, chief investment officer and head of fixed income at AllianceBernstein, "Currency-hedged global bonds have historically been much less risky than unhedged global bonds, while delivering competitive returns, as we've written before here. Furthermore, hedged global bonds have captured most of the upside of US bond returns while offering greater resilience in down markets."[1]

What's the difference between a hedged and an unhedged portfolio? A hedged portfolio tries to limit the currency risk that the portfolio has. A common strategy for hedging the currency risk is using futures contracts in the local currencies to offset potential interest-rate swings that can influence currency values. It's a bit complicated, but in a nutshell, by hedging a global bond portfolio, investors are trying to neutralize the impact that currency swings can have. This means that the investor doesn't have to worry about whether the currencies are gaining or losing against the U.S. dollar.

Figure 6.1 shows that in up markets, U.S. bonds barely outperform global bonds. In quarters with positive returns, U.S. bonds have managed 2.5 percent, while global bonds returned 2.3 percent. That means that global bonds are capturing more than 90 percent of the positive returns of their U.S. counterparts.

Where foreign bonds get more interesting is on the downside. Figure 6.1 also shows that in down quarters, U.S. bonds dropped by 1.1 percent and their global bond counterparts fell by 0.7 percent. That means that they had only 60 percent of the downside of U.S. bonds. Giddyup.

FIGURE 6.1 Global Bonds Are More Resilient
in Down Markets over the Long Term

January 1990–December 2011

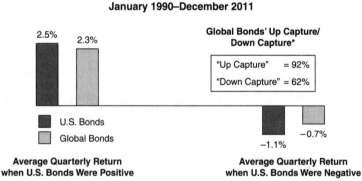

Up capture and down capture reflect the global bonds' return divided by the U.S. bonds' return over the period indicated when carried to two decimal places.
U.S. bonds are represented by the Barclays Capital U.S. Aggregate index, and global bonds are represented by the Barclays Capital Global Aggregate index.

Source: Barclays Capital and AllianceBernstein

Peebles told me in an interview that, based on these numbers, he thinks it makes sense for retail investors to put all their bond allocation into global bonds. "What difference does it make where you live?" Finally! A highly respected Wall Street strategist confirms what I've been preaching to my clients all these years.

We continued our conversation, mutually congratulating each other's genius, and came to an accord on the point that for U.S. investors who pay taxes, nothing beats U.S. municipal bonds, based on the huge tax saving that you get by investing in them. Again, consult a qualified advisor if you want munis.

You see the similar returns and lower volatility even more clearly in Figure 6.2. Over 15 years, the returns on a global hedged bond portfolio were very similar to those on U.S. bonds, but with much more stability. We have very little of the higher volatility that we see in other areas of the bond market.

FIGURE 6.2 A Hedged Global Approach May Offer Better Risk-Adjusted Returns

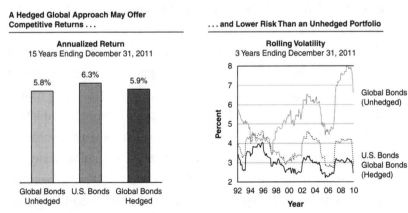

Historical analysis does not guarantee future results.
As of December 31, 2011.
Global bonds unhedged are represented by the Barclays Capital Global Aggregate USD Unhedged. U.S. bonds are represented by the Barclays Capital U.S. Aggregate. Global bonds hedged are represented by the Barclays Capital Global Aggregate index hedged to USD. An investor cannot invest directly in an index or average, and they do not include sales charges or operating expenses associated with an investment in a mutual fund, which would reduce total returns.

Source: Barclays Capital and AllianceBernstein

There are those who believe that hedging the currencies is a waste of money. I spoke to Rajesh K. Gupta, chief investment officer, and Chicky Mahtani, director of international fixed income for SeaCrest Investment Management, LLC, who said, "We do not hedge currency in our portfolios for two reasons. First, the cost of currency hedging can be quite high, especially in emerging nation economies. This is largely due to illiquidity. Second, some of the historical analysis we have done indicates that currency hedging over extended periods of time doesn't generate any additional return when all expenses of such hedging are taken into consideration."[2]

We see this in Figure 6.2. However, while Gupta's strategy is valid for institutions and for super-high-net-worth accounts, for the average retiree, the issue of volatility is paramount. Stability of returns trumps everything else for them. If hedged and unhedged global bonds end up performing similarly, yet the hedged variety do so at a slower and steadier pace, I would tell investors to go for that approach. Who needs stomach-churning, roller-coasterish volatility to end up the same place you could be by taking it easy?

We are currently living in a low-yield world, and foreign bonds and especially emerging market bonds can be a great solution for retirees. The perception is that foreign bonds are very risky, but the reality is that it really depends on which countries you are talking about. Even though the big rating agencies believe that France or Japan is safer than Brazil, I say otherwise. As I mentioned earlier, many emerging economies have become the poster children for fiscal discipline and responsibility, while Japan's economy could potentially have a debt crisis à la Greece in the not-too-distant future. France is burdened by debt, has negligible economic growth, and has an aging population, which doesn't seem too safe to me. Brazil, on the other hand, is posting strong growth, has a young population, and is becoming an economic force to be reckoned with. Investors get virtually no yield on Japanese and French bonds, but they get 7 to 9 percent on good-quality Brazilian bonds.

You don't like South America? Look at Australia. It has very strong economic fundamentals, and you can get 4 to 5 percent on highly rated corporate bonds. Throw in a strong currency and that is real income in a low-interest-rate world.

How to Invest in Bonds

There are basically three ways investors can access foreign bonds: individual bonds, international bond funds, and exchange-traded funds (ETFs).

INDIVIDUAL BONDS

When buying individual foreign bonds, you will need to convert your currency from U.S. dollars to the currency in which the bond is purchased. While you won't pay a commission, you will pay a spread on the currency. This means that while you won't see a line item that says "commission," you will not get the exact price that you see the currency trading at on your computer (the "spot price"). This is because the traders who buy and sell currencies take a spread on the spot price, which is how they profit from their services. Heads up—when you are buying foreign bonds, especially in markets that are not overly liquid, the traders will mark up the bond more to compensate for the lack of volume than they would with a more liquid bond.

Individual bonds enjoy three advantages: predictability, cost, and taxes. With every kind of bond, as soon as you lock in the price, you know exactly what will happen until maturity, as long as the government or firm is able to meet its obligations. Most bonds have a fixed interest rate, so the investor knows exactly how much income the bond will pay out on each specific date. This can be helpful in determining how much income a portfolio will generate.

The coupon of the bond (the interest that the bond pays) helps investors create a consistent income stream. When a portfolio is being specifically tailored for a retiree, these bonds make it certain how much the investor will be paid and on exactly what dates. This provides a certain comfort level to retirees.

The only cost to buy a bond is the markup that you pay at purchase. What's a markup? As with currencies, when you buy bonds through U.S. advisors, you don't pay a commission; instead you pay a slightly higher price for the bonds. Let's say that you want to buy 50 bonds, and each one is showing a price of $1,010 for a $1,000 bond. This bond was originally bought by a bond trader and is now being sold to you. Let's say you end up paying $1,015 for the bond. That means that you paid a markup of $5 per bond. This $5 goes to the broker. After that, you have no other fees. (This is if you buy the bond through a U.S. brokerage firm. If you were to open an investment account in another country, there might be a host of fees that you would have to pay. Many European investment firms will charge holding or custody fees, meaning that they will charge you to hold your security. Other charges may include paying an actual commission to buy or sell. I have seen a number of firms that actually charge a fee when you receive bond interest payments.)

Let's not forget taxes. When you own individual bonds, your cost basis is set at the purchase date, which also allows you to sell bonds if you need to realize gains or losses, or to make your portfolio more tax-efficient. You are in control of your own personal tax situation with bonds, as opposed to owning a mutual fund.

For all the advantages, there are a couple of significant disadvantages to owning individual bonds. First, you really need to understand the currency market pretty well. Yes, you may receive an extra 2 to 3 percent on a bond, but 2 to 3 percent is nothing for currency movements. If you buy a five-year bond, the local currency can move 25 to 35 percent (at least) during that time. That kind of movement will affect your portfolio a lot more than the 2 to 3 percent additional interest you are getting. How many of us are currency experts? And do you really want to spend your retirement years staring at a computer screen trying to predict what will happen between the euro and the Mexican peso?

Another disadvantage is that you need to read all the fine print on the individual bond issue (which is not always readily available in English). Some foreign bonds have different payment structures from those found in the United States, meaning, for example, that you may get back 25 percent of your principal each year for four years, or you may get 25 percent of the principal back during the first year and different amounts of principal thereafter. Some bonds may actually be linked to the U.S. dollar or to inflation (these can be very popular in countries that have been beset with runaway inflation rates in the past). Investors who want to purchase individual foreign bonds need to go into the process with their eyes wide open.

Finally, let's talk about diversification as an issue. To achieve the diversification you want and need in foreign bonds, you need a sizable retirement portfolio to begin with. Why? To achieve diversification, you need to buy enough bonds in each currency to overcome the price hurdle that comes with illiquid markets. This means that you will need to buy bonds in minimum amounts of $20,000 to $25,000, because otherwise the markups will kill you. Therefore, even if an investor holds $200,000 to $250,000 in a portfolio of foreign bonds, he will end up holding a maximum of 10 bonds total, or one or two per currency. If one issuer has financial difficulties or goes bankrupt and the price falls dramatically, your portfolio will take a big hit. Bottom line: for most clients, buying and selling individual bonds in multiple currencies probably is not practical.

INTERNATIONAL BOND FUNDS (MUTUAL FUNDS)

A reminder: as I mentioned in Chapter 5, the Patriot Act may prevent U.S. citizens living abroad from investing in certain mutual funds.

I see four primary advantages to investing in international bond funds, beginning with professional active management. In an ever-changing world, having an experienced set of hands on the wheel is critical. Knowing that the fund's manager can decide to reallocate from certain currencies to others and from country to country is a very comforting feeling for many retirees (and their advisors).

Next on the list of advantages is diversification. In the section on individual bonds, I said that an investor might need to own 10 specific global bonds, which is very little diversification. Now consider that global bond funds own hundreds of bonds, which leaves the investor with much less specific company or government risk. This means lower volatility and higher yields.

Bond funds pay out monthly interest, which is usually very important for a retiree who is trying to create a stable cash flow. Contrast that to individual bonds, which pay interest semiannually or, in many cases with foreign bonds, annually.

And finally, if you don't need to live off the income generated by the bond fund, you can have it set up for dividend reinvestment. This means that the interest earned goes back into the fund to buy more shares—a great way to build the value of the holding over time.

No investment is perfect, of course, so let's discuss the downside to bond funds, beginning with cost. Funds are paid internal management and marketing fees, and these fees can pack a wallop. Specifically, 12b-1 fees, which are partly paid to the broker, can have a severe impact on performance, especially over the long term.

Earlier I explained that bond funds pay monthly interest, and said that this is an advantage. However, you never know exactly how much to expect, which is a disadvantage. Why can't an investor predict the payment? Because the amount the fund pays is based on its holdings at that specific time. This means that if it sold some higher-coupon bonds and replaced them with lower-coupon bonds or if some of the higher-coupon bonds matured, then your cash flow would drop. This doesn't happen with an individual bond, where, unless it is classified as a floating-rate bond, the cash flow will be constant throughout the life of the bond.

Many prospective bond investors will be surprised to learn that there is no guarantee of principal in a bond fund, even though there is a guarantee with individual bonds. An example will illustrate this, but first you must understand bond premiums.

What's a bond premium? Most bonds are issued for $1,000 each. A bond trades at a premium because the bond is in demand. For example, let's say you purchased 25 Nestlé bonds for a premium price of $25,750. At maturity, you will get back $25,000 (in addition, of course, to all the interest paid to you while you were holding the bond). The $750 is the bond premium.

Why is there a premium to start with? Let's say the Nestlé bond has a coupon of 5 percent annually. In today's low-interest-rate environment, a 5 percent annual interest payment is in demand, which pushes the price up.

Back to the example of how you can lose principal in a bond fund. Sticking with those 25 Nestlé bonds, let's look at what would happen if your bond fund purchased them at the same premium. If the price of those bonds begins to drop, the value of the bond fund will drop as well. It will drop because interest rates have gone up, so a 5 percent return isn't as attractive as when rates were lower.

If you get into a time period when the prices are continually dropping, the principal in that bond fund will also continually drop. Bond funds have no maturity date; they just keep on rolling. This means that if we were to hit a period of rising interest rates, the value of the bonds held would fall in price, and so would the value of the fund.

Why would this happen? For the immediate future, this is not necessarily a risk, but in the medium to long term, the risk becomes more acute. After more than 30 years in a bond bull market, interest rates have hit bottom. Within the next year or two, it's reasonable to assume that rates will start moving higher. In a rising-interest-rate environment, there's a good chance that bond funds will lose money.

Also, mutual fund investors of all stripes need to always keep on eye on the fund manager. If the reason you chose a certain fund was that you like the manager (her track record and experience as well as her investment philosophy), and if that manager leaves, the reasons that you made the purchase to begin with may no longer be relevant. In short, you may need to find a new fund.

Finally, investors who buy into a fund are on the hook for capital gains that were generated by the fund, even if they were generated before the investor bought in. This means that you are paying for someone else's gains, while you may actually be sitting on a loss. How does this work? Let's say you bought the PIMCO Long-Term U.S. Government Fund on February 2, 2013. Let's say that in the first month of 2013, the fund manager started to lighten up on his positions because he was worried about a possible rise in interest rates. After more than 25 years of a bull market in bonds, there's a good chance that he's sitting on hefty capital gains. Unfortunately for you, by the time you buy the fund, he no longer owns a chunk of these bonds, but you're going to get saddled with a big capital gains distribution bill because of the appreciation in the fund's holdings. You didn't take part in the appreciation, yet you're stuck footing the bill.

EXCHANGE-TRADED FUNDS

As with all exchange-traded funds, a major advantage that they have over mutual funds is price; they are much cheaper. The internal fees can be anywhere from 0.25 to 1.25 percent less than those for a mutual fund. That means that over many years, an actively managed fund would have to put up some pretty impressive numbers to outperform the ETF.

ETFs are liquid, unlike mutual funds, which trade only once a day. ETFs trade throughout the trading day. I consider this to be a great advantage.

Also, ETFs are much more tax-efficient than mutual funds. Your cost basis is calculated from your purchase price, and because ETFs are passive, except for updating the index, there is little in the way of capital gains tax. This is another advantage.

There is an inherent danger of overtrading when you use ETFs for stocks and bonds. In short, just because you can trade them cheaply doesn't mean that a trade should be executed. There are tax considerations that can make such an itchy-trigger-finger approach downright foolish.

For major indexes like the S&P 500, ETFs perform almost step for step with the index. But when you get to more exotic indexes, there is a variance that can really affect an investor's portfolio performance. According to a report in the *Wall Street Journal*[3] in 2009, ETFs overall missed their benchmarks by 1.25 percentage points. The miss was most felt in less liquid markets. The *Journal* observed, "On the other hand, the $40 billion iShares MSCI Emerging Markets Index ETF returned 71.8% in 2009, lagging the 78.5% return for its benchmark by 6.7 percentage points. The $3.7 billion SPDR Barclays Capital High Yield Bond ETF posted a return of 50.5% versus 63.5% for the index it tracks, trailing by about 13 percentage points."

In lay terms, the *Journal* makes the point that investors who thought they were linking themselves to the index were surprised to learn that they didn't even come close to the return of the index.

The nature of many foreign indexes, especially those for emerging market bonds, means that ETFs can't really even track the index they are trying to mirror because the specific assets aren't available. Douglas Peebles and I discussed whether to use ETFs or mutual funds for foreign bonds. Here's his take: "When you take emerging market or global debt, put it in an ETF, and give the illusion that this is a liquid market when it's not, you mask the turnover costs associated with investing in these markets from spreads and markups. Also, no ETF is going to give you a passive investment in these markets; even Vanguard, which specializes in passive investments, doesn't do it. You can't replicate the index because most of the bonds in the index are not available to be bought. Active management actually works in fixed income, especially in emerging markets."

Aside from the fact that the ETF can't buy everything in the index, which is Peebles's point, a portfolio manager can also wade through the garbage and buy the good bonds in these small markets. This obviously is very important. Okay, do-it-yourselfers, are you prepared to take that on?

Emerging Market Debt

I want to now focus on what I believe is the most interesting sector in the foreign bond space, and that is emerging market bonds. As I have pointed out, emerging economies have been leading global economic growth and should continue to do so for the foreseeable future. They have very low debt levels compared with developed Western countries, and while they may have a bit more short-term volatility from day to day or week to week, over the long term they have performed very well and are a great way to enhance a retiree's income.

Tom Lydon of ETF Trends says, "Currently, emerging market bonds on average provide 4.75% more yield than U.S. Treasuries. Additionally, emerging debt offers diversification qualities beyond the normal fixed-income assets."[4] This is huge for investors who are looking for more income. Highly rated Brazilian bonds pay a whole lot more, as they are in the 8 to 9 percent range.

Aside from the juicy yields, we are in the midst of a transformation of the relationship between the developed world and the emerging world. If you look at how Standard & Poor's rates bonds, you will see that the United States, Japan, France, and Italy have all had their ratings cut in the last few years. Other than the United Kingdom and Germany, that's pretty much the major portion of the developed world. Now quickly hop on a jet and head south or east, and all you will see is ratings upgrades. That in itself tells the story of how we are in the midst of an economic shift that is still in its infancy.

Investments Your Advisor Doesn't Cover

We have spoken about stocks and bonds, but we need to spend some time discussing some alternative investments. Clients constantly ask what they can do outside the basic stock, bond, and mutual fund choices, but when you hear "alternative investment," perhaps something exotic like art or wine comes to mind. Never fear, retirees; I'm not going there. We're talking about real estate, private equity/venture capital, and foreign currencies here.

REAL ESTATE

The most common question I receive is about real estate, so we'll start there. Unlike many advisors, who are out to protect the assets that they handle and often try to dissuade clients from investing in real estate, I love real estate now. For investors with enough money to invest in a nonliquid investment, take a look at the asset class.

Why? Buy low and sell high. For many investors, this strategy is hard to implement because it's supremely difficult to know when you've hit an ultimate peak or valley. Sometimes, however, simply knowing that something has dropped a lot is sufficient. Take, for example, U.S. real estate. After such a serious fall, can prices keep dropping? The answer to this question is a resounding maybe! But for an investor, that question may be less relevant. While it is virtually impossible to pick the exact low price of any asset, it is possible is to buy a high-quality asset at a huge discount. This is buying low. When I can buy assets at 30 to 40 percent off their prices of a few years ago, I get interested. Imagine what would happen if Walmart or Macy's advertised a 40 percent off sale on everything in the store. There would be lines around the block.

U.S. real estate markets have been crushed. With prices in some markets 30 to 50 percent lower than they were a few years ago, real estate seems to be cheap. I am certainly not saying that we are out of the woods; prices could continue to trend lower. But when you consider that the Federal Reserve has publicly and repeatedly committed to keeping interest rates low, and that mortgage rates are still at record low levels, there could be a huge upside. Please note that U.S. real estate is very much localized, and while some locales are a mess, others are starting to see prices move higher. Yields on rental properties are nothing to sneeze at, with 5 to 7 percent yields being common in good markets.

For those of you who are looking to start getting involved in real estate, here are four ways to go about doing it.

1. *Investment property.* Go out and buy some rental or commercial property. As an individual property owner, you are in control. You decide when to buy or sell, how much rent to charge, and so forth. There are a few negatives to an individual buying an investment property, however. A common problem that many individuals face is raising the large amount of money needed to get started. The high initial investment means that most beginners are able to purchase only one property, and this lack of diversification enhances the risk involved in the investment. There is also the headache of being a landlord and having to deal with leaky faucets and burst pipes. I would caution retirees with less than $1.5 million to invest that they should probably get their exposure to real estate in a different way. Real estate isn't terribly liquid, and for retirees with smaller nest eggs, the lack of liquidity could become painful. I have a lot of clients who have 80 to 90 percent of their net worth tied up in a single property. They may have a very respectable net worth, but keep in mind that if you need a quick 50 grand, you can't go out with a saw, cut off a spare bedroom, and hand it over as payment.

2. *Real estate investment trusts (REITs).* A REIT is a trust company that raises a sum of money to buy, develop, manage, and sell real estate assets. By purchasing one unit of a REIT, you are purchasing a part of a managed real estate trust, providing much greater diversification. REITs are similar to investing in regular stocks, so there is no prohibitive minimum investment. Since they are publicly traded on major stock exchanges, they provide relatively quick liquidity. In addition, REITs are normally required

to distribute 90 percent of the income that was generated from their real estate holdings. This way, you receive your rental income without having to fix the plumbing!

3. *Limited partnerships.* There are many people out there peddling real estate deals. For a reasonable investment, you become a limited partner in a group that is going to buy a building, a strip mall, or some other property, the price of which is well beyond the average person's means. A note of caution: You need to perform due diligence on the deal itself and the people behind it to make sure they are honest. We all know stories of fraudulent real estate deals. Be thorough. Unless you know the people very well and they have a track record, stay away.

4. *Related stocks.* Ask your financial professional for stocks that are related to the real estate market. These may include publicly traded roofing, landscaping, and lumber companies, to name three. These companies have the potential for price appreciation if we see continued momentum building in the construction industry.

Nontraded REITs

One asset class that has started to gain attention for both the right and the wrong reasons is nontraded REITs (NTRs). NTRs are investments in REITs that don't trade on any stock exchange. Unlike publicly traded real estate, NTRs don't have the same fluctuations in principal that you find in other REITs.

NTRs have become popular because they distribute a high level of income, usually in the 7 percent range. Many investors who want exposure to a beaten-down U.S. or European real estate sector like NTRs because not only do they get a well-diversified real estate portfolio with a big yield, but they also get the potential for capital appreciation in the real estate held. We started seeing real estate companies buy NTRs for significant price premiums in late 2012. NTRs usually build 2 percent annual rent increases into their leases, and these are mostly passed through to investors, providing an inflation hedge. NTRs are required to either liquidate or list their shares on an exchange within a specified period, usually at least seven years.

NTRs may sound too good to be true; after all, who would devise an instrument that gives investors a 7 percent return, potential capital appreciation, and no fluctuation in the share price? Critics of NTRs point to the very high fees paid by investors, which ultimately bring down returns, and the lack of transparency in pricing these assets. I have seen NTRs that charge anywhere between 6 and 15 percent as an up-front fee, which is a pretty sweet deal for the broker who's selling it to you. You may be struggling to generate income for your retirement, but that broker making the 6 to 15 percent fee is going to be sipping lots of drinks with umbrellas in them during his worry-free retirement! Also, just because there is no fluctuation in the share price doesn't mean that the actual value of the instrument hasn't moved; rather, it's probably the case that no one knows how to price it. NTRs are required to update their net asset value 18 months after their offering, and if you look at their reports to the SEC, you will find that some share prices have dropped well below their initial prices.

Michael McTiernan, a lawyer for the SEC, told the *New York Times,* "One common sales tactic we object to is the suggestion that they are eliminating volatility simply because they don't tell you what the value is. It's not that it's not volatile. It's just that you don't know."[5]

Firms like American Realty Capital and others have taken these criticisms to heart and are launching products with daily pricing and much lower fees. These firms are legit, and while I sound like I am very anti-NTRs, I acknowledge that they have a place in some portfolios as a solution for today's nonexistent interest rates.

PRIVATE BUSINESSES

For many retirees, the concept of investing in private companies is a big turnoff. After all, most of us have been approached by a friend of a friend or a distant relative with a great idea that will revolutionize the world as we know it. It will take a $50,000 contribution from us, but it's a home run and we will quadruple our money in six months. For almost all retirees, the answer to these approaches should be an absolute *no*.

Traditional private equity has been controlled by the very wealthy, and for retail investors, a minimum investment of $500,000 is required. Wealthier retirees can allocate 5 to 10 percent of their net worth to private equity deals, but with a $500,000 minimum investment, an investor would need a $5 to $10 million portfolio. Even if you have that kind of money, consider that with half a million dollars in one deal, you're not getting any diversification.

Once again thanks to technology, the whole world of private equity and venture capital is becoming democratized. What started with the Nobel Prize–winning concept of microfinancing, which allows a good-hearted person to lend a small sum to help, for example, a female entrepreneur in India, has turned into "crowdfunding." What is crowdfunding? It's gathering a group (or crowd) of individuals to pool their money in support of a cause or a business.

Some start-ups[6] have brought crowdfunding to the world of private equity by creating a platform through which entrepreneurs can raise money from less traditional sources, while giving retail investors the ability to invest in private companies with realistic sums of money. This opens up a sector of the investment world that was once the province of the ultrawealthy.

How do crowdfunding sites work? I'll use OurCrowd as an example, since I know it best. First, the management team performs due diligence on all prospective investments. Considering that this firm is headed by veteran leaders of the Israeli high-tech revolution, as well as a former Goldman Sachs analyst and the head of technology investment banking at Lehman Brothers in Israel, chances are that the due diligence is solid. Once an investment meets due-diligence requirements, it is listed on the platform, where individual investors decide whether or not to get involved by investing relatively modest sums (as compared to other private placements). In many cases, $10,000 to $20,000 is all that's required. This business model is the height of transparency, compared to the more classic private equity model that requires an investment of a million dollars in a fund that is probably closed for seven or eight years.

In full disclosure, I actually worked as an analyst at Israel Seed Partners, the venture capital firm that OurCrowd founder Jon Medved created. With my background in venture capital, I am very cynical about its usefulness. Venture capital firms don't provide much value to the companies they fund, other than writing very large checks, yet in exchange for the lack of value added, they are given a 25 to 40 percent equity share of the company, and they take huge management fees from their investors, even if they have a terrible track record. Crowdfunding private equity does an end run around both private equity and venture capital firms, while benefiting both the companies' founders (who keep a greater percentage of their companies) and investors (Joe Smith can invest in a high-tech start-up and can actually pick which one he wants to back). I think it's likely that the success of crowdfunding will lead to a reform in the current private equity and venture capital business models.

I was fortunately able to interview Jon Medved on the crowdfunding movement. Medved is the founder and CEO of OurCrowd, a better way to invest in start-ups. According to the *Washington Post,* Medved is "one of Israel's leading high tech venture capitalists." In the September 2008 *New York Times* Supplement "Israel at 60," Medved was named one of the top 10 most influential Americans who have had an impact on Israel. Medved has invested in more than 100 Israeli start-up companies, helping 12 of them to get to valuations in excess of $100 million.

JON MEDVED ON CROWDFUNDING

Q: Can you explain crowdfunding as it pertains to investing in start-ups and why there is a need for it?
Medved: The current funding model isn't working. It takes less money to get a company off the ground, leaving a capital vacuum left by larger institutions. So, from the start-up's point of view, it needs to move faster and requires less money than what venture capitalists can provide.

From the investor's point of view, we've had a lost decade of returns in the stock market. Returns for the foreseeable future aren't that compelling. Investing a small amount of money in a big idea with huge potential provides the upside in portfolios right now.

Crowdfunding pools together small amounts of money from a group of people to make a particular investment. It started with simple donations on sites like Kickstarter, and now crowdfunding companies like OurCrowd enable accredited investors to invest in the equity of start-ups in increments as low as $10,000.

At OurCrowd, we're a bit of a hybrid investment platform—we're not a venture capital firm because our investors have complete discretion as to which investments they make and how much they invest. But we're also not an open crowdfunding marketplace—we're doing real due diligence, and only a fraction of the start-ups that apply appear on our website. We also invest our own capital in every deal we open to the crowd.

Q: For higher-net-worth retail investors, do you think there is a place in a portfolio for these types of investments?

Medved: There's always a place for start-ups in a well-diversified portfolio. It's high-risk, but start-up investing shouldn't be done with play money. The same portfolio management rules hold true for investing in start-ups as for stocks that are publicly traded. Good security selection and proper diversification are key to making money this way. The Kauffman Foundation's research showed that people who invest in start-ups via groups (like what happens in crowdfunding or angel investor networks) achieve returns of 2.6 times their capital over three years. That research looks even better when investors own a diversified portfolio of 12 start-ups.

Q: The potential for scams in this abounds. How do you assure your investors that you really are showing them good deals?

Medved: It can be a problem. Start-ups don't have the same financial reporting responsibilities as publicly traded companies do. So, in open crowdfunding marketplaces, there is a chance that fraud could occur. The thought is that when you open a deal to the crowd, the collective wisdom should sniff out shams.

To help mitigate this problem, at OurCrowd, we spend considerable time and effort curating our deals, choosing just a small percentage of the companies we meet to appear on our website. We perform a due-diligence process that's robust enough for us to invest our own capital in these companies before we ever show a deal to our investor community.

Investing in private companies is certainly more speculative than buying regulated investments; they are not for everyone.

Speak with your financial advisor to see if this kind of investment is appropriate for your specific financial situation.

FOREIGN CURRENCY

Should U.S. investors own foreign currency? This is becoming a big issue in the financial planning community as new products become available and brokerage firms develop more robust trading platforms that are capable of handling multiple currencies simultaneously.

Opponents of owning other currencies would say to investors living in the United States, "Why do you need any other currency? The U.S. dollar is the world's reserve currency, so why bother with others?" They might also point out that investors holding shares of Pepsi, Ford, and other multinationals already have exposure to multiple currencies through these stocks.

Proponents of owning foreign currencies will point out that the U.S. dollar has been losing value for decades, and that foreign currencies are the best way to protect your portfolio. In addition, they will point out that currencies have become a separate asset class, like stocks, bonds, real estate, and so on, and therefore they provide investors with real portfolio diversification.

We can't discuss diversification without addressing correlation, a measure used to determine how separate assets move in relation to each other. If you have two stocks that move in tandem, then they are correlated. The point of portfolio diversification is to find assets that are not correlated, so that if something moves down, something else may move up. If you have a portfolio that is perfectly positively correlated, then you have not really diversified because everything is moving in the same direction at a similar rate.

I am a big believer in owning currency. As I have pointed out throughout this book, I have nothing against the United States, where I hold dual citizenship, but the rest of the world is gaining on America, and as it does, other countries' currencies should benefit over the long term as well. I view holding other currencies as not just a hedge against the dollar, but a very legitimate approach to trying to make money and profit in the markets. Now, I am not saying that you should leave everything else at once and become a currency trader, because that is very speculative. What I am proposing is that you take a respectful chunk of your money and diversify into a few currencies. How?

First of all, you can buy individual currencies. You can either ask your broker to help you or do it in your online account. Most firms now allow this. You will need to convert your U.S. dollars into whatever currency you want. When you start checking the value of your account after the purchase, you may see the dollar value appreciate or depreciate, because, for the sake of showing a portfolio value, the firm will probably convert the value of your holdings into U.S. dollars. If the U.S. dollar actually strengthens against your currency, your portfolio value in U.S. dollars will drop, and vice versa. I can't stress this point enough. Short-term currency movements happen, and they could cause a short-term drop or gain in the value of your assets when they are converted back into your base currency of U.S. dollars.

Buying individual currencies is not for the faint-hearted and is not for everyone, and here's an anecdote that makes my point. In one episode of the *Seinfeld* TV show, the character Cosmo Kramer, an unemployed eccentric, started showing a group of what he thought were wealthy Japanese tourists around New York City. They told him that they had 50,000 yen, so he started showing them a great time on their yen. He then enters Jerry's apartment and asks to borrow some pillows. Jerry asks why, and he responds by saying that the Japanese will be staying with him for a while. "Manhattan can be quite pricey, even with 50,000 yen," he says. Elaine responds, "50,000 yen—isn't that only a few hundred dollars?" "Evidently," Kramer replies. Study your currencies before investing in them.

Another alternative is CurrencyShares. These are basically the ETFs of the currency world. The big advantages these have over buying actual currencies is that you can buy them in U.S. dollars, meaning that you don't have to do the whole currency conversion thing. Since there's no need to convert currencies, the cost of trading them is similar to that of buying and selling any stock. If the currency is paying any kind of interest rate, then the CurrencyShares will also pay. It's like flying to Sydney, Australia, popping into a bank, opening an account, and sticking your money in a time deposit, except that you avoid a super-long flight! This is a better solution for most investors than actually buying individual currencies.

These two options notwithstanding, for most of my clients, I actually like using a global bond fund to accomplish the currency part of their diversification. I am a pretty smart guy, and I know a thing or two about currencies, but no one can be an expert in every single thing. I would rather turn my money over to an expert in currencies and let him decide which ones he thinks will be stronger and which ones will be weaker. And since he does it in conjunction with bonds, you will get a higher level of income.

It goes without saying that those of you who are planning to retire or have already retired overseas should have a very large part of your money in your local currency, because most of your expenses will be in that currency. If you convert a lot of your funds into your local currency, you won't have to worry about what happens with the dollar. You are now living in another currency, so be smart about it.

We've covered a great deal of ground in the book so far. We've taken a whirlwind tour of the world and covered a wide range of investment instruments. However, I want to caution you: Don't be like the recent college graduate with a BS in biology who thinks he's ready to practice medicine. Investing abroad can be complicated and entails several moving parts.

Next we'll discuss the most efficient and effective ways to put all these pieces together, and I'll provide you with guidelines for how to choose partners whom you might engage to accompany you along the way.

CHAPTER 7

Putting It All Together

A physician who treats himself has a fool for a patient.
—Sir William Osler

I've also seen a similar quote about a lawyer who represents himself in a court of law having a fool for a client, but I don't have an anecdote for that one. What I do have is a woeful tale of trying to be my own physician.

Before I was married and my wife could steer me in the right direction, I got pretty sick, but I didn't know what was wrong with me. I had a fever of over 101 degrees (Fahrenheit) for five days in a row and had little appetite, but, in manly fashion, I figured I would take some Tylenol and a few bowls of chicken soup and all would be well. After a week, a friend came over to visit and told me that I looked a bit yellow. I finally decided to pay a visit to the doctor, who quickly diagnosed hepatitis!

"Oops," I said. "I guess I got that diagnosis wrong." What made things even worse was that I was living with a few roommates, and they all needed to get shots. One of them had just left for a vacation abroad, so it took a while to track him down to tell him to get his immune globulin shot. Needless to say, I wasn't the most popular guy in the apartment!

Had I put my ego to one side and relied on a professional, I would have saved myself and my friends a lot of pain and inconvenience.

Does the same hold true for an investor's retirement portfolio? Is a retiree who manages her own money a fool, or is she an investor who saves a lot of money over the long term and achieves her stated goals?

While the argument over doing it yourself (DIY) versus engaging a professional rages on for younger investors, the question becomes much more acute for retirees. Statements like this from Nick Hodge of *Wealth Daily* sum up what I call the new "financial populism." Hodge says, "You have to create goals in order to pursue them. And you need a plan to avoid wandering aimlessly. Both of these things can and should be done ON YOUR OWN. I can't emphasize how important this is. The only thing a financial advisor is going to do is push you toward the funds he or she is incentivized to sell."[1]

Why do I call it financial populism? It's a classic populist movement where you blame the establishment for screwing the average person. In this case, it's blaming Wall Street and the financial advisors in its employ for being out only for themselves and shafting the little guy with excessive fees.

I am not at all against individuals managing their own portfolios; I am just against the blanket dismissal of financial advisors as being useless, and as charging exorbitantly high fees without results that justify their pay. It's just not true.

Let's discuss the best ways for individuals to manage their money, especially the international part of their allocation. Should you do it yourself, use a financial advisor, or hire a professional money manager? Or maybe use a combination of these?

Do It Yourself

Here the client is his own manager, so to speak. There is plenty of information online that can help an individual create basic asset allocations, based on age, and figure out how much money he will need for retirement. If you go this route, you will open an account with an online broker and pay less than $10 per trade with no management fees. As long as you are disciplined and don't overtrade, this is going to be the cheapest way to invest.

A factor in favor of DIY is that you have the luxury of staying in cash if you get nervous. Professional managers often have a mandate that they must be fully invested. Obviously there are times of intense volatility when many retirees just want to move to the sidelines and wait things out, but if they are using a professional manager, this becomes more difficult.

If you have a straightforward financial profile, or if you have more income than you need from social security, pensions, and other investments, you can do your own research and manage your own money. You can use a combination of exchange-traded funds (ETFs), index funds, and individual stocks to match the allocation that you can find online. Basic websites like Yahoo! Finance offer stock and mutual fund screeners where you can input certain criteria and then get results based on those criteria.

For investors looking for idea generation, have a look at Seeking Alpha or StockTwits. There you have a whole community of both professional and recreational investors giving their analysis of stocks and ETFs. The fact that a stock, mutual fund, or ETF showed up on one of these sites, however, doesn't relieve you of doing your own homework to decide if it's an appropriate investment for you. It gets trickier for the international side of your portfolio.

If you just want mutual funds or ETFs, then there are plenty of resources, like Yahoo! Finance, Morningstar, and Seeking Alpha, to name a few. The choices are a lot fewer if you are looking for an individual foreign stock. The best resource I have found, and one that I use, is Financial Visualizations (finviz.com). It has fantastic stock screeners for virtually all global markets. It's a very robust platform, and if you have the ability to really know what criteria you want when choosing a stock, this is for you.

In my years in the business, I have seen hundreds if not thousands of DIY retirees' portfolios, and in many cases, they are a mess. That's probably why these people come to me; the individuals who are managing their portfolios successfully don't need an advisor.

AVOID THESE MISTAKES

No Strategy

I often see portfolios that are a hodgepodge of stocks that the investor must have bought after watching weekend business shows or spending too much time listening to friends talk about their stock picks while on the golf course. There is no rhyme or reason to the portfolio; it's just a haphazard combination of stocks. After speaking to the client, it becomes clear that more income is needed, yet the portfolio includes virtually no income-producing investments.

It's easy to buy an investment; it's much tougher to sell. But buying and never selling anything is not a strategy.

No Tax Efficiency

Usually DIY portfolios have major losses that have not been real-
ized because these investors are notorious for never selling their
losers, and often pull the trigger and sell their winners way too
early. I can't begin to tell you how many accounts I see where
the investor is on the hook to pay a ton of capital gains taxes,
yet with a few basic moves, she could eliminate a good share of
them. Don't get sucked into the famous retail investor mantra
that says, "I'll sell it when it goes back up." That's not a strategy.
That's just an emotional and arbitrary response. Investors should
forget about the past and always look to the future. Ask yourself, "What stock gives me the best chance to profit?" If it's your
loser, so be it. If there is something better, cut your losses and
move on.

If you have sold positions and now are sitting with capital
gains, review your portfolio to see if you have any positions that
are currently at a loss. While many investors would never consider selling a position that is losing money, selling your losers
can actually make you money.

Never think that all is lost. Some good can actually be derived
from losing stock positions. When the position is sold, the investor realizes the loss, which has certain tax advantages. The loss
can be used to offset other gains, thus lowering the tax bill. In
fact, for many investors, tax-loss selling may be the most important way to reduce their tax bill. If this is done correctly (be sure
to speak to an accountant before making any trades), it can save
the investor money.

For example, if a person has a gain in Stock A and he decides
to sell it, he will be taxed on that gain in full. But if he has a loss
in Stock B that he realizes by selling it, he can take the amount
of the loss and offset it against the gain in A, drastically reducing
the amount of taxes he owes. This might not recover the entire
loss, but it certainly cushions the blow.

Conversely, if you have substantial losses from previous years, you should speak to your accountant at once to see if it pays to sell positions that have gained in value in order to cushion any future tax bill. By doing this, the investor can actually reset her cost basis at a much higher level without incurring any tax liability. You have until the end of each year to implement these strategies.

There is a rule in the United States called the wash-sale rule by which the IRS disallows the deduction of a loss from the sale of a security if a "substantially identical security" was purchased within 30 days before or after the sale. Let's say you sell 100 shares of Microsoft on December 23, 2013, at a loss and buy back those 100 shares of Microsoft on January 15, 2014. In this case, the loss deduction would not be allowed. The wash-sale rule is designed to prevent investors from making trades for the sole purpose of avoiding taxes.

Lack of Knowledge of Products Available

For many retirees, enhancing income is their number one priority. Unfortunately, when you rely on the financial media in planning your portfolio, they will usually end up convincing you to own a basket of index funds, and you are likely to fall short of the income you need. Most individuals are limited in their understanding of what's available in the market that will enable them to achieve their goals.

I once met with a 77-year-old widow. She had $800,000 in a bunch of low-cost index funds at Vanguard. To her credit, she was very much on the ball and understood how markets worked, and she repeatedly told me that she had read about the need to use only low-cost index funds. She was receiving about $20,000 a year in social security, and she owned her home worth $500,000. She had no other assets and no other sources of income. She loved to travel and visit her three children and ten grandchildren, who were spread out across the globe. She very much wanted to leave her home and her investment account to her children as an inheritance.

She had done a very thorough job in tackling her expenses, so she knew she needed $50,000 a year, which meant that her investments needed to generate $30,000 to make up for the gap between her need and social security. Her index funds were generating about $16,000 a year in income, which meant that she was drawing down principal. Now, you may say, what's the big deal? Even if she takes $30,000 a year, she has plenty of money to live a very long life and still leave something to her family. However, she was adamant about wanting to leave at least that $800,000 to her children and grandchildren.

I started asking her whether she knew anything about investing internationally in both stocks and bonds, and whether she knew about preferred stocks. She said that she had no idea what preferred stocks were and that she was under the impression that she had enough international exposure through her S&P 500 index fund, as all the big U.S. multinationals do significant business abroad.

Allow me a brief commentary at this point. The "father of indexing," Vanguard founder John Bogle, preached that investors should buy and hold Vanguard's low-cost index funds. He became incredibly wealthy as his investing mantra was widely adopted by the public as an almost biblical mandate. Unfortunately, he is the only one who got truly wealthy. His followers got a sock full of coal. Where is the criticism of him for encouraging investors to buy and hold for life and subjecting his followers to a "lost decade" in which U.S. markets have barely budged? All I can say to his followers is that at least they didn't pay high fees.

Back to our story. I explained to her what could be done with her portfolio to increase income generation (basically by using assets that are available in the marketplace, nothing speculative—

it wasn't as if I was recommending wheat futures) so that she could generate the income she needed and still grow or at least protect her principal. She was blown away because in 90 minutes I had contradicted everything she had been reading and watching on television. She was literally shaken, and she said she needed to go home and think about it. A week later, she called and said she had decided to open an account with half her money to see if what I was saying was truthful. A year later, she transferred the other part. I certainly earned my keep.

Not Enough Time

Let's face it. You worked hard for your nest egg, and now that you are retired, you want to enjoy your retirement. How many of you want to take the time needed to follow the markets, monitor your investments and potential investments, and make sure that you are positioned to accomplish all of your retirement goals? To really keep on top of things, you need to spend a few hours a week. If you love investing and you enjoy putting in this much time or even more doing your homework, then go for it. But the majority of retirees don't have much interest in following the markets and their investments. They are busy doing a host of other activities, and they want to outsource the handling of their money to a professional. For those who plan on doing a lot of traveling, I think that it becomes that much harder to stay on top of things because you are out of the loop. Yes, I know you can bring your laptop or even your smartphone with you, but it's just not the same. Let's say you travel to Europe. U.S. markets will be open in the afternoon and evening in local time. Chances are you are not going to waste your afternoons and evenings hanging out in a hotel room, logging on, and buying and selling stocks.

Buying High and Selling Low

I spoke about the impact that emotions have on the investing process. Another mistake investors make is that they tend to buy the same stocks that everyone else is buying. This can create a situation in which they are buying after the stock has already moved up aggressively. The goal for an investor is to buy low and sell high, not the other way around.

Forbes recently reported on a 2006 study in which behavioral economist Professor Terrance Odean found that "like children fighting over the same toy, investors are often attracted to stocks because others want them. In fact, individuals are much more likely to buy and sell the 10% of stocks mentioned in the news and ignore the other 90%. The problem with buying stocks when they're popular rather than on the basis of fundamental value is that they tend to be expensive and susceptible to changes in investor sentiment. The day after a stock ranks among top performers, two-thirds of all trades by individual investors are buys (institutions, by contrast, tend to wait for dips in prices and trading volume). Over the following month these hot issues underperform the overall market by an average 1.6 percentage points."[2]

This is not an issue that's specific to retirees; it's just that, as with many of these problems, it's more magnified with retirees because whatever they managed to save is what they have. They don't have a lot of potential earning power, so each big mistake can really affect their ability to have enough money with which to live out their lives.

Overtrading

Another mistake investors tend to make is that they trade way too much. It's very difficult to always be right when you're trading stocks actively. In fact, if you trade too much, instead of investing in a company, you are basically gambling on the direction in which a stock will move. I am familiar with a lot of people who have told me that they trade "just to make a hundred dollars a day." They say that it's pretty easy to make that kind of money, and the extra $26,000 that they can make will provide them with all the supplementary income that they need. Inevitably, after about two weeks, they give up on that strategy. Why? Because it's not successful for the overwhelming majority of individuals. If it really was so easy to make that kind of money every day, don't you think everyone would be doing it?

Getting Old

Obviously this is not a mistake that investors make; rather, it's something that nature imposes. This really gets overlooked by the proponents of DIY. We should all live long lives, with good health and mental clarity. The problem is that at some point, the retiree is going to start to have memory issues, a bit of forgetfulness, and a general slowing down of his decision-making facilities. While this doesn't impede his having a fulfilling retirement and is by no means cause for him to be sent off to an assisted living facility, it does raise the question of whether it may cause damage to his investment portfolio.

I have a client who's in her eighties and still likes to actively trade stocks. She decided that she would give me the bulk of her money, but keep about $100,000 with an online brokerage so that she could, in her words, "play a little." Well, about a year and a half ago, she read an article about AutoZone and decided to buy it. The problem was that she entered the wrong symbol and bought the wrong stock. Now, I'm not trying to kid you; mistakes happen to everyone. I have also entered incorrect symbols, but she indicated that this was happening somewhat frequently, and that she just kept the stocks. When an advisor makes this kind of faux pas, he can get the trade canceled, and the client ends up buying what was intended. If there is some kind of loss involved, the advisor will eat it. That doesn't happen when you are investing on your own.

Step 1, 2, 3 . . .

When it comes to investing in foreign markets, much of what's available in the United States is also available abroad. Investors can purchase individual stocks, bonds, mutual funds, and ETFs no matter where they live. This means that the issue isn't one of availability; rather, it's how to go about buying foreign securities.

Investors could open up bank accounts in foreign lands, transfer dollars to fund those accounts, have those dollars converted to the local currency, and then buy stocks. Another option would be to transfer money in the same way, but hire a local money manager to manage the funds in the particular local market. In my experience, this method is just not practical for most retail investors. Many hedge funds and other institutional investors follow this process; they actually open up trading accounts in individual countries and use those accounts to buy and sell foreign securities. That may be good for multibillion-dollar operations, but there aren't very many retirees that I am aware of who would actually send their money overseas and have some manager there manage their money. In many cases, doing so requires speaking the local language, and there are all kinds of tax and cultural differences, not to mention different time zones. It's not a great solution.

As a result of technological innovation, most brokerage firms and online firms like Fidelity, E*TRADE, Schwab, and TD Ameritrade offer some sort of foreign offering, although it's not too robust. (Interactive Brokers is probably the best firm around if you are planning on investing globally.) Some of these firms allow you to buy only foreign stocks that trade in the United States (American Depository Receipts, or ADRs, which we covered in Chapter 5). Others limit their scope to a few major markets. If you are a DIY investor, chances are that you won't have a clue as to how to go about buying these securities. Chances are that your brokerage won't offer too much, anyway. If you work with an advisor, there is a better chance that his clearing platform will have a larger offering. My firm clears through Pershing, a Bank of New York Mellon company, and we have access to 55 markets throughout the world. Now that is robust. There aren't too many markets where we can't trade.

Keep in mind that trading in foreign markets can be quite costly. In addition to commissions, which are almost universally higher than in the United States, you may also have to pay stamp duties, taxes, clearing fees, and exchange fees. Don't forget currency conversion costs of around 1 percent of the size of the transaction. Buying foreign stocks on local markets isn't a cheap proposition. Still, a good investment is a good investment, and to refrain from pulling the trigger because of costs doesn't make sense.

If you are going to go it alone, there is a big responsibility that falls on your shoulders. You need to understand and stay current with a myriad of currencies, and do your own stock research. Without a doubt, investing globally has its advantages, but without a full understanding of the various products and how to research them, you may be selling yourself short and end up doing more harm than good.

FALLOUT FROM THE PATRIOT ACT

I was once surveying the dessert table at a wedding when I got a call on my cell phone. The caller sounded frantic, and when I explained that I was at a wedding and couldn't really speak to him (I didn't want my hot chocolate cake to get cold!), he said that he couldn't wait for me to call him back the next day. So we spoke as my cake cooled (such sacrifices I make). He told me about the call he'd just received from his broker at a well-known firm in the United States, saying that he had to either close out his account or transfer the account to another firm. Coincidentally, I knew the broker, and I called him. He told me that he had just received a memo saying that most accounts with less than $250,000 in assets that didn't have U.S. addresses had to be either closed or transferred within two weeks.

Some firms have created special divisions and forcibly transferred clients' accounts to these new divisions, even if doing so severed a longstanding relationship with their brokers. I once met with someone who had been working with the same Cincinnati, Ohio, advisor for 36 years and got a letter saying that his account had been transferred to a new advisor in Houston, Texas.

Why the change? Since the terrorist attack on the World Trade Center, U.S. firms have taken a very strict approach to non–United States–domiciled accounts. With the Patriot Act and other new laws, it has become much more difficult for these firms to accept accounts from U.S. citizens living abroad, and many firms have just decided that they would rather not put themselves into this situation and have taken the step of either not taking any new business or setting up a new division to deal with these accounts. While brokers on these accounts have fought tooth and nail to keep their clients, the compliance departments have won out, and this is their solution.

The broker who I was speaking with in this case also told me that of the 50 or so accounts that he needed to dispose of, about 30 belonged to children of immigrants who were born in Israel and speak hardly any English. This is not just a U.S./Israel issue. It applies to all U.S. citizens living abroad, whether they are in London, Panama, Singapore, or Costa Rica. Where they are just doesn't make a difference.

The issue of children having accounts in the United States that their parents set up is a common one that I deal with. This broker said to me that most of these children don't even know how to dial the United States, let alone handle a conversation about their finances in English. They would have a hard time trying to access the money that has been put aside for them. Not only that, but their new advisor in the United States doesn't know them and is unfamiliar with their long-term goals and needs.

What should you do if you're a U.S. citizen living abroad? I would recommend going local. I would find an advisor who is licensed both in your new country of residence and in the United States to handle your accounts. Not only will this professional be attuned to life in your new country, but she will also speak your language and in general be able to make things much easier going forward.

In addition, someone who is local who has an arrangement with an American firm will not have the same problems with not being able to buy certain investment products. He will have all the compliance in place, allowing the client to have access to the wide array of investment choices that she has come to expect.

MIMICKING

The conventional wisdom is that investing is stacked against the little guy. It says that the best investors in the world have a big advantage, and it makes no sense to even try to compete with them, so throw up your hands and buy index funds or ETFs. This isn't exactly accurate. There have been a bunch of financial start-ups that give investors the ability to link themselves to the exact portfolios managed by the world's very best investors.

Covestor allows retail investors to actually link up to any money manager on its platform and buy his portfolio in your own account. According to CEO Asheesh Advani, "Covestor brings the clarity and efficiency of an online marketplace to the world of money management. Investors can compare and select from a transparent marketplace of money management talent that includes over 100 professional portfolio managers and successful individual investors. Covestor's Portfolio Sync technology automatically replicates trades, providing clients the convenience of 'set and forget' functionality and the protection of Covestor's proprietary trade filtering."[3]

This means that the investor can keep all of his money in his own name, in his own brokerage account and have someone of his choosing manage his portfolio with total transparency. Another advantage is that there are no entrance or exit fees and no loads, and the firm provides the clients with a high level of service. If one manager is not to your liking, you can go ahead and replace her with another manager on the platform. This gives an individual control over the type of portfolio that he wants invested.

Another start-up that I just love is called AlphaClone. AlphaClone also allows investors to link up to the best money managers in the world, but it has a different approach. It is able to track the public holdings disclosures that hedge funds must make. It then creates certain models that track these moves by the successful hedge fund managers, and these have proved to be very successful portfolios.

INTERVIEW WITH MAZIN JADALLAH, CEO AND FOUNDER OF ALPHACLONE

Q: Can you explain how AlphaClone works?

MSJ: We use SEC public holdings disclosures to derive "virtual fund of funds" strategies that seek to leverage the intellectual property of established hedge funds. We can do this because funds that manage more than $100 million must file their holdings quarterly with the SEC. Our firm specializes in tracking and analyzing these funds through their disclosures. Our research shows that managers tend to have longer holding periods than most people perceive. The average holding period is about one year. We also have shown that hedge funds tend to generate their performance from their long positions much more often than most people would think. Finally, our proprietary research platform gives us a long historical data set that allows us to test the efficacy of following a manager's disclosures over a long period of time. Simply put, through our platform, we have a pure view of the manager's long selection skill unfettered by the use of leverage, shorts, or trading strategies—we call this a "Clone Score."

Just as with any successful fund of funds program, the key to our success begins with manager selection. Even though our strategies ultimately invest directly in the disclosed positions of the managers we select, our methodology seeks to select managers and not their holdings. Our process then seeks to mitigate risk in its many forms. We combine multiple managers into any one strategy so as to mitigate performance risk, blowup risk, fraud risk, style risk, and data or filing risk. We employ a process called dynamic hedging in our strategies that seeks to allow our strategies to run long during generally increasing markets and be well hedged during generally decreasing markets. In this way, we can mitigate systemic market risk while still maintaining an aggressive long-only posture during rising markets. Ultimately we seek to give the investor top-quartile (not average) hedge fund returns at lower overall volatility than the market over time.

Q: There is a knock on disclosure-based investing that by the time you read the filings, it's too late. How would you respond?
MSJ: Our research shows that the lag in disclosure doesn't really matter. We looked at the performance of all Top 10 Holdings clones for each manager in our universe between 2000 and 2011; about two-thirds outperform the French/Fama broad market factor and

40 percent outperform by 400 basis points annualized over the period! The lag isn't as significant as most people think.

I have employed some of these strategies for clients, and the results have been off the charts. That's not to say that past performance is indicative of future results, but the past results have been impressive. They take the arguments of conventional wisdom—that is, that professionals have the game stacked in their favor—turn them on their head, and actually piggyback on these successful investors. I once was telling another financial professional about this, and he said that it didn't seem right to piggyback on someone else's investments. I said to him, "Huh? Do you call your clients and recommend that they purchase a certain stock? Where do you get the idea from, an analyst from Goldman Sachs or a talking head that makes an appearance on Bloomberg TV? You are piggybacking as well." Here you are using publicly disclosed filings to determine what stocks to buy and sell. These hedge fund managers have very impressive long-term track records, and now, with technology, you can actually own the same portfolios as they do.

These may be great ways to invest your money, but you need to take a step back before you implement any strategy. I may sound like a broken record, but randomly buying off-the-shelf products isn't a retirement planning solution. Rather, it's one-size-fits-all investing. In 90 percent of the cases, it's the exact opposite of what retirement investors need. Retirees need a plan to achieve the goals and meet the needs that they have. And believe me, each person has different needs and goals. While you share a hobby with your fishing buddy or symphony companion, your financial situation and outlook are different, and an advisor can help drill down and create a blueprint to help get you where it is that *you* need to get to, not where your friend needs to be.

FEE-ONLY FINANCIAL PLANNERS

So it's clear that I really feel that for most retirees, self-managing a portfolio without outside help is a mistake. For investors who nonetheless want to self-manage their money, but who wouldn't mind some objective advice, there is the option of using a fee-only planner.

I once spoke to a friend who had her money at TD Ameritrade. She was pretty sure that she was doing a good job of managing, but she wanted some impartial advice. She also asked if there was a way to incorporate her other investment (real estate) into the overall advice that she sought.

Many investment advisors and financial planners have begun to offer clients consulting services as well. The client pays the advisor an hourly fee to consult on the entire investment portfolio. The advisor will analyze the stocks, bonds, mutual funds, and other investments that the client is holding and also get a thorough understanding of the client's risk profile and short- and long-term goals, and give objective advice on the holdings.

The primary benefit of a fee-only advisor is that, because the advisor is getting paid at an hourly rate only, she can provide objective advice. Such advisors are better able to look at your entire financial situation without being swayed by any personal benefits that may arise from giving certain recommendations. In fact, most of these advisors will provide free referrals to other professionals that the client may need (such as accountants or lawyers).

There is a common myth that in the financial industry, you need to have millions of dollars before anyone will pay attention to you, let alone give you top-level service. The beauty of fee-only consulting is that it levels the playing field. The advisor charges the same hourly fee to a multimillionaire and to a newly married couple with limited financial means. That new couple will receive the same level of attention as anyone else because there is no difference to the advisor; he will make the same amount of money from the hourly fee.

There are certain types of retirement accounts [401(k)s] where the investor needs to make the investment choices, but the money is locked up somewhere and cannot be moved into a normal brokerage account. In many cases, the investor loses substantial amounts of money because the money wasn't invested correctly. Many investors with these accounts should seek the counsel of a fee-only advisor and make sure that this retirement money is invested correctly.

With the popularity of online investing, many people have taken it upon themselves to manage their own portfolios. While they enjoy managing their own money, many of these people would like to receive supplementary advice, or a second opinion, on whether what they are doing actually makes sense. Fee-only advisory services are the perfect solution for this problem. The advisor will sit with the client, work on an allocation model with her, and go over all potential investments, and then the client can go home, enter the trades herself, and continue managing the portfolio on her own. Many fee-only advisors will send reminders to DIY clients to come in for quarterly, semiannual, or annual meetings to help keep them on track.

For those who insist on handling their own finances, I strongly recommend meeting with a fee-only advisor just to make sure that you are on the right track. With a few meetings a year, you still retain control of your own account, but you get a second opinion. Of course, like everyone else, fee-only planners are human, and while they should be looking out exclusively for their clients' best interests, inherent in their profession is a relationship that could lead to dependency. They want you to keep coming back for those meetings because that's how they are remunerated. Just make sure that you set up meetings when you need them.

For those who don't want to manage their own money, there are a few different options. The first is turning your money over to a pro.

USING PROFESSIONAL MONEY MANAGERS

With all the financial information that investors are bombarded with, it has become much harder for them to manage an investment portfolio that meets their needs. Many investors have thrown up their hands in despair and started to look at using professional money managers. They want someone who has his finger on the pulse of the market, can wade through all the information, and can make decisions as needed without having to contact the client.

In the past, professionally managed investment accounts were only for the ultra-rich investor. While tycoons such as Bill Gates or state pension funds had access to these money managers, they were generally off limits to the average investor, as initial investments of $10 to $20 million were the norm. However, over the last five to ten years, advances in technology that automate portfolio management have made managed accounts accessible to and increasingly popular among investors who don't necessarily have the millions that were once required. Because of these advances in technology, minimum account sizes today can be as low as $50,000.

One important advantage of having a managed account is that the portfolio manager has discretion over the account. This means that she can make decisions without speaking to the client first, which can be an advantage when a decision needs to be made quickly. In the more classic model of a broker and client relationship, the broker needs to get the client's approval before initiating any transaction. The problem with this is that the time it takes to obtain the client's okay can often be costly, especially if the client is not easy to reach.

There are two ways to choose a money manager. The first is to go directly to a firm that specializes in this field. While this is possible, it's important to keep in mind that there are more than 20,000 professional money managers in the United States alone. Where would an individual even start his research?

The other option is to work with a licensed investment advisor via a brokerage firm. Many brokerage firms have research teams whose sole area of expertise is analyzing portfolio management firms, and they provide their investment advisors with lists of the top-rated portfolio managers. One advantage of using a brokerage firm is that these firms often have special agreements with the portfolio management firms, enabling clients to use the managers with relatively low minimum investments, often in the $50,000 to $200,000 range. Another advantage of using money managers through a brokerage firm is that the advisor is able to oversee the manager that the client is using. If the manager fails to perform as she should, or if there has been a change of management at the firm, your advisor can relay that information to you, and you can switch managers at no cost.

Managed accounts usually charge an annual fee, called a "wrap fee," that is based on the amount of money under management. Generally, all the portfolio manager's trading costs are included in this fee. This puts the client and the manager on the same side of the table and eliminates any conflicts of interest that a manager may have that arise from selling products and receiving commissions for them. As the value of the account goes up, the manager makes more money; conversely, if the value drops, the manager makes less.

For investors with more specific needs, using a professional money manager may not be the best solution. Whatever manager you choose will have a specific mandate and will invest that way. If you pick a manager who is a U.S. large-cap manager, he is going to invest in large-cap American companies, and he won't waver from that. While you get the exact same portfolio as a Bill Gates would, it comes with a downside, and that is that there is no personalization and customization. The manager is not going to change his entire model and strategy in order to make you happy just because you need to generate a certain amount of money to live on.

Using professional managers is also the most costly approach. If the manager is accessed through a broker, it can cost anywhere from 1.2 to 2.5 percent annually. Now, I am a big fan of not cutting off your nose to spite your face. These managers provide a very good service and your trading costs are included in the fee, so for certain types of accounts, this is a very good solution.

WORKING WITH AN ADVISOR

Financial advisors help clients to evaluate their entire financial situation, then determine whether the total portfolio will work to make sure that the clients can reach their long-term goals. The results are often surprising. It is quite common to find a client's overall wealth situation to be skewed toward either very aggressive or too conservative investments. A client who receives stock from her company can often have a third or more of her wealth tied to this particular company. By taking a comprehensive view of their clients' financial situation, advisors can help create diversification strategies and asset allocation approaches that will help the clients achieve their long-term goals intelligently. A good financial advisor can act as your own personal chief financial officer (CFO). He can take a full view of your entire financial situation and make sure that everything is doing what it's supposed to be doing. If you have multiple accounts, in order to prevent redundancy in your portfolio, someone needs to sit on top and get a full view. That's a role of the advisor.

Financial advisors also act as sounding boards for retirees. You can bounce various ideas off of your advisor and see whether they work out economically. Sometimes an advisor can think of issues that you may not have thought about and that are crucial in making a correct decision.

I once met with a single lady in her late sixties. She was a semiretired writer who would submit articles for publication a few times a month. She had about $400,000 in her portfolio, rented a small house, spent about $35,000 a year, and had about $25,000 in income from her social security and what she made from selling her articles. She told me that her dream was to buy a small home in southern France where she could go for two weeks a year to write and enjoy the country. When I asked her whether she would rent out the house to tourists for the remaining part of the year, she hesitated before saying no. She said she hated the thought of others living in her home. She was worried that buying the house would make too big a dent in her savings and that she should give up her dream. I told her that there are plenty of places to rent in southern France, and that I thought she would be way ahead of the game if she rented one of them for two weeks instead of buying a place, as she wouldn't have to pay the cost of upkeep of a place that she owned.

In terms of costs, she would keep her principal and just need to generate a bit more income, which we would accomplish by moving a lot more money into foreign stocks and bonds, which yield much more than their U.S. counterparts, as I have showed. She called me a few days after our meeting and was so happy that she could have her dream of spending time in this very beautiful part of the world and just write. Left to her own devices, she would never have been able to work out a way to fulfill her dream.

The current market volatility has investors revisiting the value of professional portfolio management and financial advisor expertise. Professional financial advisors have a wide range of tools available to help investors navigate the rough investment waters and create portfolios that can weather the storm. They can keep you on track to help you reach your long-term goals.

For investors who still want to retain control of the handling of their investments, using an advisor may be ideal. After all, the advisor works in cooperation with you, and together you can come up with a plan for success. The investor has the final say on all decisions; it's just that there is someone else in the picture to help guide him and make sure that he gets the whole picture.

Professional advisors provide two main benefits to individual investors. First and foremost, the advisor should become a counselor, helping her clients determine what their long- and short-term goals are. While this may sound simple, most clients have multiple goals and need multiple strategies to achieve them.

Next on the list of advisor benefits are the technical aspects of asset allocation and portfolio management. For many retirees, the most pressing issue may be how to save enough money to live out their life without going broke. But this isn't the only goal. Retirees often focus entirely on one goal and overlook other important issues, like helping their children, giving more money to charity, and traveling. Investors often have many sources of investments that go beyond their personal investment portfolio, such as checking accounts and social security, pension plans, rental properties, and so on.

Not all advisors are created equal. If you will be investing more and more funds globally, then you need to work with someone who is an expert in the field of global investing. It doesn't stop there; you also need an advisor who works on a brokerage platform that will enable you to accomplish what you are setting out to do. You don't want to work with someone who is unable or unaware of how to purchase foreign securities.

Case Studies for Implementing the GPS Retirement Strategy

Let's revisit our friends from Chapter 1 and see what means and methods I would recommend to them as they reach and pass their retirement parties.

AADI AND VANITA: WORKING WITH A FEE-BASED FINANCIAL ADVISOR

First, we had the electrical engineers Aadi and Vanita, who live in a Boston, Massachusetts, suburb. With the exception of Vanita's 10-year hiatus while she was nurturing their two preschool children, they worked for the same company for nearly 40 years and are 3 years into retirement. They are fortunate to have both a defined-benefit pension and a 401(k), but the company has discontinued health insurance for retirees. Their children are married with families of their own; they are financially self-sufficient and will receive the proceeds of the couple's life insurance policies.

In addition to a mortgage-free home and $125,000 in savings, Aadi and Vanita own an apartment building that is currently valued at $5 million, but with a commercial loan balance of just under $2 million that is due in the next two years. The property generates sufficient income to pay the balance of the loan. Through a planned giving program, they have pledged the building to an organization that builds medical facilities in rural communities in India. The agreement includes a provision that up to $500,000 of the value can be diverted to their needs, but they are committed to leaving the entire value with the charity. They spend their time helping this organization reach out to other Indian expatriates who are in a financial position to help with its humanitarian work. This involves a moderate amount of travel, which they enjoy.

Aadi and Vanita have enough income to live comfortably in retirement, but Aadi's recent heart attack has made the couple appreciate the need to allocate some of their retirement nest egg to cover healthcare expenses throughout the rest of their lives.

Aadi and Vanita are fortunate to be set up with solid pensions and social security, as these by themselves might provide enough for them to live on. Knowing that they're going to get a substantial amount of income from their property once the loan is paid off is a huge bonus. Once this kicks in, they're going to need to decide what to do with all that money. It's probably going to be one of three things or a combination: enhance their lifestyle (travel more), increase what they give to their children and grandchildren, or take the extra money and either give it to the Indian medical facilities program now or let it grow and leave it to the program posthumously.

Regarding their 401(k), they could roll it over into an IRA. Generally investors have a lot more choices in an IRA than in a 401(k). Many 401(k) plans don't give investors a wide array of investment options. In many cases, they provide very basic offerings that are broad-based and don't provide a lot of choices for investing in the United States, let alone have a robust international offering.

Aadi and Vanita are busy with their volunteer work. Do they have any interest in managing their own money, or would they prefer a hands-off solution? It seems to me that they would want it to be hands-off because they want to commit their time to their philanthropic work. Nevertheless, I'm going to suggest that they go to a fee-only planner who can create an asset allocation model for them that they can implement, then meet with that advisor twice a year to review the investments. They don't need anything very customized because they have much more money than they will ever need. They would pay the advisor an hourly rate, then go ahead and execute the plan.

Based on a defined-benefit pension, social security, and the boatload of income from the property, their cash flow is sufficient. They don't have a lot of issues that are calling out for help. The real issue is what will happen when they get older and can't carry out the plan any longer. The fee-only planner can provide them with more help as they become feeble. Perhaps the planner will put them on retainer and guide them through the system.

Aadi and Vanita should set up an account with an online broker, buying the ETFs or index funds that they need there. If they don't want to choose the funds themselves, all of these firms have platforms offering managed ETF or mutual fund accounts. These are off-the-shelf products that are managed according to the brokerage firms' models. These cookie-cutter products are tailor-made for this couple, as they invest in a basic allocation that's very broad based. They're low cost. Aadi and Vanita don't have to do anything.

A typical Madison Avenue asset management firm will take 1.5 percent a year versus 0.5 percent for the managed portfolios that the brokerage firms offer. This is a good place to mention that there now are actually fully licensed online asset managers (virtual asset managers). They have various asset allocation models based on client risk profiles. They use low-cost ETFs, and they don't believe in a lot of trading, which keeps trading costs down. Betterment.com is an example of this kind of firm.

Aadi and Vanita have the setup that many retirees daydream about, but with proper planning, Lincoln and Doris can also achieve their retirement goals.

LINCOLN AND DORIS: WORKING WITH
A FINANCIAL ADVISOR

As a reminder, Lincoln and Doris have been blessed with six children, all living near their parents in Charlotte, North Carolina. Since their children and now their grandchildren have always been the center of their lives, they want to provide for them as best they can during their retirement. When one of the kids needs orthodontics, her grandparents pick up the tab. Sundays are always spent around the large dining room table, and the grandchildren are now spilling over into the family room at card tables. Lincoln and Doris never miss a grandchild's dance recital or soccer game, and they plan to take each grandchild on a trip to a foreign country of the child's choice to celebrate his high school graduation.

Doris, who is 62, is a medical social worker at a hospital and would like to reduce her hours significantly; Lincoln is an accountant, but not a partner in the firm, and at age 64, he is ready to retire. They will spend about $60,000 on themselves and their family yearly. While they have social security benefits of $35,000, they must make up the difference from the $1 million in their IRAs and 401(k)s. This means a balancing act of capital preservation and lifestyle choice so that they will not need to liquidate their paid-for home worth $500,000 for many years to come.

The first question I have for Lincoln and Doris is whether they have yet begun to take social security benefits. This is a topic of great dispute in the financial planning community because the longer they hold off, the greater the benefits they will get. It's important to check www.socialsecurity.gov for eligibility and benefits. Currently, full retirement age is 65, 66, or 67, depending upon your birth date, with lower benefits if you start taking it younger and increased benefits each year you wait to claim benefits up to age 70.

I would ask them whether Lincoln can hold out until he's 66 and how much Doris wants to scale back her hours. If Doris is thinking of taking social security, she can't work too many hours. If Lincoln can hold out for two years, the enhanced benefit might make a big difference. If he wants to retire right away, we could make it work.

If they get benefits of $35,000, they will need another $25,000 annually from their $1 million portfolio, which is not a difficult mission. Lincoln and Doris have other issues to consider, however. If, for whatever reason (bad investments, huge expenses, or plain old bad luck), disaster strikes and they blow through all their money, their fallback position would be to liquidate the house. For many retirees who are worrying about running out of money before they pass away, their home is a saving grace.

There are those out there who preach the advantages of taking a reverse mortgage, including the director of the Center for Retirement Research at Boston College. Academics may be fans of reverse mortgages and believe they are the way that many retirees will make it through retirement, but if you do a web search on reverse mortgages, you'll see a slew of scams and cries for regulation. I'd rather see you sell the house outright and live in a rental property than get taken to the cleaners with a reverse mortgage.

Another important consideration is what Lincoln and Doris want to do in retirement. Even though they want to give to their families while they're still living, they need to be careful not to over give, or they will run the risk of depleting their nest egg. Do they want to maximize what they leave to the family or just leave whatever is left? Do they want to generate even more money while they are living and give it to the family while they are alive to see them enjoy it? If they play their cards right and end up with average investment returns, they could have quite a bit of money saved and may want to think about giving part of it to charity as well.

They need the classic financial advisor because they have so many moving parts. In a case like this, the advisor will get to know the children as well. It's important to plan the transfer while everyone's healthy and thinking clearly.

Lincoln and Doris are the classic fit for the GPS retirement portfolio because they have enough money to meet their expenses, but they could use extra income, and extra income from the portfolio would be welcome while they are living and would be put to good use after their deaths. Over the next 20 to 30 years, not only will they receive an enhanced income and cash flow, but they will have the ability to grow their portfolio with a 50 percent exposure to foreign markets, which are poised for the strongest growth.

While right now they spend $60,000 on themselves and their family, they may want to spend more as their grandchildren age: "small kids, small expenses; big kids, big expenses." They may want to help pay for their grandchildren's college educations and weddings in 10 to 15 years. By working with an advisor, they can plan for those things well ahead of time. A good advisor will be able to anticipate these desires in a way that Lincoln and Doris can't. Having $1 million is nice when you need to generate only $25,000 a year to live, but when you begin tapping into it, you can draw it down too fast. By working with an advisor, they can avoid that.

How can they find the right advisor? They need to find one with global expertise—one who has invested in multiple currencies throughout the world. They should interview advisors until they find the right one. In addition to the standard interview questions, they should ask about geographical expertise and available products. The advisor may try to say what they want to hear, so they need to prepare by reading and by asking for a couple of references to clients who are similar and who invest globally. Obviously the advisor will give clients he is close to. Once you get to the level of references, even if the reference says what the advisor has led you to believe she would say, you can see the wobble points.

Advisors charge in different ways. The standard or "classic" model, as I like to call it, is based on transaction costs. When you make a trade, you pay a commission. If you don't do anything, you don't pay anything. This method is becoming outdated, and a clear trend toward fee-based advisors has taken hold. The advisor will charge an annual fee based on assets, and in many cases all transactions will be executed at no costs. There are variations on this model, with some advisors charging an administrative fee and a small ticket charge "commission" on transactions to cover costs. The advantage of this model is that it puts both the client and the advisor on the same side. In the classic model, there's an inherent conflict of interest. Maybe the broker is a good guy, or maybe not. When the client gets a phone call advising her to liquidate Microsoft in favor of Google, you don't know if the broker is advising this because he thinks it's in her best interests or because he really needs to make two commissions (one to buy and one to sell). Does he have an upcoming tuition payment that he needs to generate commissions to pay? There are plenty of ethical advisors; I'm just pointing out the inherent conflict of interest.

Generally, administrative or fee-based accounts like this cost between 0.5 and 1.25 percent, depending on the firm and the portfolio.

Why the trend to the fee-based model? To align the interests of the client and the advisor. The client wants to make money, and so does the advisor. The more the client makes, the more the advisor makes. Thus, the client knows that when the advisor calls to suggest a change, he is doing so because he feels that it's in the client's best interests and is really a good idea. Since he makes nothing on the transaction, it would be a waste of time for him to suggest a trade unless he thinks it's a profitable idea.

Whenever I explain fees, everyone always says, "I want to pay only if I make money; why should the advisor get paid if I lose money?" That's a logical question. The regulators allow that kind of commission schedule only in very limited cases and for people who have incredibly high net worth and substantial income, called "accredited investors." The reason the regulators don't like this fee arrangement is that it gives the advisor an incentive to recommend only investments that will be home runs, not what is in the investor's best interests. If the advisor gets only a percentage of the profits, she doesn't care about clients making 2 to 3 percent because there's little in it for her. She will then be overly aggressive for these clients, and that's what the regulators don't like.

RUTH: GOING IT ALONE

Now let's look at a woman of more modest means and see what I'd recommend for Ruth, in Indianapolis, Indiana. She's 56 with three grown children. Two of her children are married with families of their own, but her youngest daughter, like so many other people the world over, has had difficulty launching her independent life.

Ruth is willing to be frugal for the rest of her life. She raised her three children with very little help from her ex-husband. While she has a $900 mortgage payment on her $150,000 house, she should have it paid off around the time she retires from her job as an office manager in a medium-sized business. She will need to work until age 66 to meet her retirement goals.

Ruth's living expenses are about $40,000 each year. Social security will kick in about $20,000, and she has an IRA worth

$200,000 and another $200,000 in an individual account. She would love to spend time traveling the United States and enjoying time with her family. She wants to save as much principal as possible so that her children will be in a better position to help her grandchildren with the proceeds of her estate. She will have no life insurance after retirement.

Conventional wisdom says that when someone retires, she needs 75 percent of her preretirement income to live on. If this were true, Ruth would need $30,000, but I don't go with that. My basic formula is that leisure time equals money spent. I've yet to sit with a retired client who sits in a cafe, goes to a show, and travels and still spends less than he did when he was working. It just doesn't happen. I counsel my clients who are planning for retirement to keep the level of expenses at the very least equal to, if not more than, the amount they spent before they retired.

I don't know anyone who spends significantly less in retirement. I understand that the house will be paid off, but there are so many other expenses that it doesn't work out. That 75 percent number is used for everybody, including the 25 percent who've retired with less than $50,000 in savings. This 75 percent rule is taken as a given in financial planning circles, and it's just not accurate.

While at first glance it would appear that Ruth may have some cash flow issues in retirement, her situation is not too bad. Why? While her spending won't go down and may even rise a bit, she will have paid off the mortgage on her home, and her $900-a-month payment will evaporate, thus dropping her expenses by almost $11,000 a year.

Ruth has an advantage because, although once she retires in 10 years, she'll spend more money, but because of the paid-off mortgage, she'll have an additional $10,000 each year and a paid-off home. She'll still need to generate $10,000 over social security, but if she invests correctly and contributes to her IRAs, in 10 years her current $400,000 should be worth a minimum of $500,000 (and that would be a lousy scenario) and significantly more if she uses the GPS portfolio strategy. If she has $500,000, she can preserve her principal and leave it plus the house to her children.

As a frugal person, Ruth has always managed her own money, not seeing the value in paying an advisor. She's using an online brokerage, and she does her homework. She has always stuck to a mix of low-cost index funds and ETFs and has always preferred dividend stocks. What she needs to keep an eye on is not getting overly conservative or aggressive in her investments as she nears retirement. As she approaches retirement, she needs to ease off the gas pedal and get a more conservative portfolio. To learn more about how ETFs work and what new products are available, she can look at www.etftrends.com. Sites like www.seekingalpha.com also have good ETF information and generate lots of ideas that an investor can work through to match her own goals and preferences. It has good information for dividend investors and a number of bloggers who cover that style of investment. Ruth might also be interested in www.stocktwits.com because it's a community of investors giving their own take on investing. StockTwits is like the watercooler of the investing world.

The next 10 years are a bridge for Ruth. During these 10 years, it is critical that she amass wealth so that she will get up to that minimum level of $500,000. Anything above and beyond that is a huge bonus. She does need to be careful not to be overly aggressive because if the market drops significantly, it will cause a huge drop in the value of her portfolio, and she won't have enough time to make the money back. She should have a goal that, at a minimum, she should retire with $500,000 in her IRA and individual accounts.

RICHARD AND NANCY: WORKING WITH
AN INTERNATIONAL ADVISOR

Finally, let's revisit the would-be adventurers, Richard and Nancy. Appliance salesman Richard and self-employed bookkeeper Nancy have raised their two children and put them through college, and they are now ready to retire and see the world. The high school sweethearts will qualify for their full social security benefit next year and have been researching countries that they'd like to retire to. They're using the Association of Americans Resident Overseas website to research and plan their move. The AARP also has information that they've found useful. Costa Rica may be the first country they try.

Their financial goal is to make sure that they have enough money to live on, estimating their expenses at $40,000 annually. Their savings are modest for retirees, a total of about $200,000 from savings, an inheritance from Nancy's mother, and small IRAs. Richard served in the Army right after high school and receives a small disability income for a bad knee. Their Portland, Oregon, home has a $10,000 balance on a tax value of $250,000, which was partially paid from the inheritance that Nancy got from her mother. They are willing to live in a rental home if maintaining their home becomes a burden or if they need to liquidate it in the future to fund their lifestyle. They will rent the house to others while they are living abroad, hoping that their rental income will cover the maintenance costs and taxes and contribute a little something to their cash flow.

Their combined social security payment and VA disability compensation is $30,000, and they figure that they can live abroad for $40,000. This means that they need to generate $10,000 from their $200,000 nest egg. They're another good candidate for the GPS retirement portfolio because it will enhance their income.

Without the GPS retirement portfolio, if they were to keep all their money in dollars while they were living abroad, they might have $200,000, but if the dollar were to fall 20 percent, that would make a big dent in their retirement plans. It's essential that they have non-U.S.-dollar exposure to protect the value of their portfolio in local terms. The GPS retirement portfolio provides the currency hedge because 50 percent of the money is invested outside the United States, protecting it from a drop in the dollar; it also makes generating $10,000 on their investments easier.

They really need to work with an advisor who knows currencies and who has a clientele of retirees who've retired abroad. Country-by-country nuances can affect tax liabilities, the amount of money that can be brought into and out of the country, and other issues.

They might want to ask their friends or fellow members of AARP and the Association of Americans Resident Overseas which broker or advisor they're using. They should not attempt to go it alone. Some investments, most notably mutual funds, will be off limits to U.S. citizens living abroad. Internet connections may be spotty. An annual fee model will be most appropriate for them. They will spend 1 to 1.5 percent on management fees. They will not want a transaction model, because, as I have mentioned, trading foreign securities and currencies can get costly.

Americans planning to live abroad may make budgets based on what the locals tell them they need, but in my experience, Americans have higher standards of living, which blows their estimates. The Panamanian local doesn't care about keeping up with ESPN, so she doesn't need a satellite dish and service. And even though Richard and Nancy are retiring abroad, don't forget those annual trips back to the United States to visit the family. I often see retirees abroad who forget to include this in their budgets. After living abroad, they can move back to Portland on their $200,000 nest egg with a paid-for home.

LIVING ABROAD

Retirees living abroad who are living off their investments need to get their holdings compatible with their new financial situation. While your money may all be in U.S. dollars, your living expenses will be in a foreign currency, and therefore you need to protect the purchasing value of your money in local terms. For example, in Israel three years ago, during a six-month period, a retiree with $1 million would have seen the value of his portfolio drop to $800,000 simply because of currency movements. Don't make the mistake of many immigrants who came with what they thought was enough money, only to be hit by a strong currency and be left scrambling to find extra sources of income to live on.

I can't stress the importance of being realistic. I once knew a couple who lived in New York and decided to retire in Israel. Part of their plan to make ends meet was to stop traveling entirely and work a bit in retirement by tutoring children in English. There were only two problems with their plan. One was that they still had a child living in Denver who was married with three small children. For some reason, they convinced themselves that the child and grandchildren would visit them twice a year. Needless to say, that didn't happen, and after a year of never seeing their grandkids, they gave up and started traveling. However, they never budgeted for it, and by the time they called me, they were blowing through their savings. Their master plan of becoming part-time English tutors was also short-lived, as they decided to move into a community of mostly seniors, so the need for English tutoring was nonexistent. I succeeded in stabilizing their financial situation, but not without taking a machete to their expenses. Why did this happen? Because they never bothered to do their homework to see whether their plan was feasible.

I'll close the book with a story of hope and inspiration for anyone who thinks his financial plans will not materialize. A client of mine was widowed when her two children were still in elementary school. Fortunately, she lived in a home that had been bequeathed to her, but that was her only financial advantage. She received survivor benefits from social security and a part of her husband's pension. She worked as a freelance writer, hardly an occupation known for getting rich quickly. Nevertheless, with determination, she managed to take her boys with her on an annual hiking trip to India while setting aside a nest egg. She became my client in 2004, telling me that her first priority was to take care of her children in the event that she died before they "launched" their lives. Her second priority was to leave them enough money to launch their lives in style.

Four years later, the financial meltdown brought her into my office, and we rebalanced her holdings. Things got worse, and we kept rebalancing. To her credit, she stuck with me and I with her. We used the GPS retirement portfolio strategy, and she made a financial comeback.

She wanted to invest in real estate, and I encouraged her to do so (a financial advisor with a client's best interests in mind won't try to steer him away from a worthy investment). She now had two investment apartments. She later downsized and took the money from the sale of her inherited house to buy a third apartment. Whenever we met, she was apprehensive that her holdings would be insufficient, but she was sitting on more than $1 million in overall holdings—on a freelance writer's income, no less.

Fast-forward to the fall of 2012, when she called me after a visit to the doctor, where she had received the devastating news that she had incurable cancer. We reviewed everything, and I worked with her and her lawyer to pave the way for her children, now in their early twenties. When she passed away some six weeks later, she left them $120,000 cash and three properties worth $1.2 million in trust to provide income. When her children are both in their thirties, the trust will liquidate, and they can take the balance and launch their lives very well indeed.

The world is in a constant state of change. There's a global economic rebalancing taking place before our eyes. A new breed of economic leaders is on the horizon. Take advantage of it! Investing in the new world will provide you with financial security in *your* lifetime if you're smart about it and use the right advisors.

Forget your past mistakes. Refocus your energies based on what you have and where you should be going. Since I'm a freshmen-level expert on *The Old Man and the Sea*, I'll leave you with a quote from Santiago, who was fretting over equipment he didn't have:

> *Now is no time to think of what you do not have.*
> *Think of what you can do with what there is.*
> —Ernest Hemingway, *The Old Man and the Sea*

I invite you to visit the website I developed specifically for readers of this book: GPSinvestor.com. You can subscribe to updates there and read what I've written about the news of the day and how it affects my thinking about my clients' portfolios.

Budget Worksheet

MONTHLY BUDGET

A. Monthly Expenses

Fixed Expenses	Amount	Utilities	Amount	Variable Expenses	Amount
Rent		Phone bill		Vitamins	
Mortgage		Cell bill		Bank/credit charges	
Property tax		Electricity		Buses	
Taxes (federal & state)		Gas		Taxis	
Childcare		Water		Car expenses	
Tuition fees		TV/cable		Entertainment	
Private classes		Internet		Cigarettes	
Travel to work				Lottery tickets	
Travel to school				Restaurants	
Charity		**Other Expenses**	**Amount**	Movies/shows	
Newspapers/ magazines				Baby items	
House cleaning				Medicines	
Car lease					
Savings plan				**Supermarket**	
Medical insurance				Grocery	
Life insurance				Fruits/vegetables	
Gym membership				Fish/meat	
Homeowner's insurance					
Car insurance					
				Total Monthly Expenditures $	

MONTHLY BUDGET (continued)

B. Monthly Income

Salary/Wages	Amount	Other Sources	Amount	Other Sources	Amount
1.		Social security			
2.		Unemployment benefits			
(Husband)		Dividend income			
1.		Interest			
2.		Royalties			
(Wife)		Rental income			

Total Monthly Income
$

C. Monthly Balance

Total Monthly Income		Total Monthly Expenditures		Monthly Balance
$	−	$	=	$

ANNUAL BUDGET

D. Annual, Holiday, and Occasional Expenses

Occasional Expenses	Amount	Holiday Expenses	Amount	Annual Expenses	Amount
Extracurricular activities		Gifts		Medical	
Car testing and licensing		Food		Dental	
Tuition fees				Heating/gas	
Summer camps				Car maintenance	
Day camps				Clothing (parents)	
Vacation				Clothing (children)	
				Shoes (parents)	
		Other Expenses	Amount	Shoes (children)	
				Plumbing repairs	
				Electrical repairs	
				Home improvements	
				Painting	
				Parties	
				Charities	
				Total Annual Expenditures $	

E. Annual Income

Miscellaneous Income	Amount		Bonus	Amount
			Total Annual Income $	

ANNUAL BUDGET (continued)

F. Annual Balance

Total Annual Income		Total Annual Expenditures		Total Annual Balance
$	−	$	=	$

G. Total Annual Balance

Monthly Balance

$	× 12 = Annual Balance	$	Final Annual Balance
	Total Annual Balance	$	$

OBLIGATIONS AND LOANS

A. Debts and Payments Due

Owed To (Taxes)	Amount	Owed To (Utilities)	Amount	Owed To:	Amount
Credit card debt		Electricity		Postdated checks	
Income tax		Telephone		Medical expenses	
		Cell phone		Dental expenses	
		Gas			
Mortgage		Water			
Rent		Property tax		Other	
		Cable			

OBLIGATIONS AND LOANS (continued)

B. Debts Owed to Organizations and Private Lenders

Loan Fund/ Lender	City	Amount	Single Payment Date	Monthly Payment	Remainder

C. Total Debts

Total Debts

$

D. Total Guarantees

$

E. Loans Owed to You

Borrower	City	Phone	Amount Owed

Investment Criteria for International Markets

Investment Criterium		Stable Political Environment	Economic Freedom	Young population with growing middle class?	GDP Forecast	Diverse Economy
Country/ Region						
	China	−	−	+	+	+
	India	−	−	+	+	+
	Asia	+	+	+	+	+
	Asian Tigers	+	+	+	+	+
	Australia	+	+	+	+	+
	ASEAN	+	+	+	+	+
	Japan	−	+	−	−	+
	Brazil	−	+	+	+	+
	Colombia	+	+	+	+	+
	Peru	+	+	+	+	+
	Middle East	−	−	+	−	−
	Africa	−	−	+	+	−
	Israel	+	+	+	+	+
	Turkey	+	+	+	+	+
	Europe	−	+	−	−	+
	Scandanavia	+	−	−	+	+
	Canada	+	+	−	+	+

Notes

Chapter 1

1. "The SunAmerica Retirement Re-Set Study: Redefining Retirement Post Recession," 2011, http://www.agewave.com/research/retirement resetreport.pdf, accessed January 6, 2013.
2. "Global 500: Our Annual Ranking of the World's Largest Corporations," *Fortune*, 2011, http://money.cnn.com/magazines/fortune/global500/2011/countries/US.html.

Chapter 2

1. Genesis 11:1–9.
2. Capital Management Resources Ltd.
3. Ron J. Patton, Faisal J. Uppal, Silvio Simani, and Bernard Polle, "Monte-Carlo Reliability and Performance Analysis of Satellite FDI System," *Mechatronic Systems*, Vol. 4, Part 1, October 31, 2006, http://www.ifac-papersonline.net/Detailed/25211.html, accessed January 3, 2013.
4. Gerald S. Martin and John Puthenpurackal, "Imitation Is the Sincerest Form of Flattery: Warren Buffett and Berkshire Hathaway," April 15, 2008, http://ssrn.com/abstract=806246 or http://dx.doi.org/10.2139/ssrn.806246, accessed January 3, 2013.

Chapter 3

1. "2012 Index of Economic Freedom," New York: Heritage Foundation, 2012, http://www.heritage.org/index/country/peru, accessed January 3, 2013.
2. Homi Kharas, "The Emerging Middle Class in Developing Countries," OECD Development Centre Working Paper No. 285, January 2010, http://www.oecd.org/social/povertyreductionandsocialdevelopment/44457738.pdf, accessed January 3, 2013.
3. Ewen Cameron Watt, Fiona Ellard, Imran Hussain, Jeff Shen, Richard Urwin, and Sam Vecht, "Are Emerging Markets the Next Developed Market?," BlackRock Investment Institute, August 2011, https://www2.blackrock

.com/webcore/litService/search/getDocument.seam?venue=PUB_IND&source=GLOBAL&contentId=1111146576, accessed January 3, 2013.

4. Chung-in Moon, "Market Forces and Security," Annual Symposium on the United Nations System in the Twenty-First Century, United Nations University Headquarters, Tokyo, Japan, November 8–9, 1996, http://archive.unu.edu/unupress/marketforces.html, accessed January 3, 2013.

5. Edwin J. Nijssen, Susan Douglas, and Paul Bressers, "Attitudes Toward the Purchase of Foreign Products," NYU Stern School of Business, May 1999, http://pages.stern.nyu.edu/~sdouglas/rpubs/attitudes.html, accessed January 3, 2012.

6. E-mail interview, November 5, 2012.

7. Dion Friedland, Magnum Global Investments Ltd. website, http://www.magnum.com/About.aspx?RowID=40&GroupName=DionArticles, accessed January 6, 2013.

8. Polya Lesova and Michael Molinski, "Latin America's New Tigers Forge Ahead," *MarketWatch*, July 25, 2012, http://articles.marketwatch.com/2012-07-25/markets/32829627_1_credit-ratings-peru-colombia/3, accessed January 7, 2013.

9. Toni Peters, "Colombia 2011 GDP Up 5.9%," *Colombia Reports*, March 22, 2012, http://colombiareports.com/colombia-news/economy/23013-colombia-gdp-up-56-statistics-agency-.html, accessed January 7, 2013.

10. Securities and Exchange Commission, "International Investing," http://www.sec.gov/investor/pubs/ininvest.htm.

Chapter 4

1. Larry Kudlow, "Washington Is Going the Wrong Way," *Kudlow's Money Politics* (blog), *National Review*, July 10, 2009, http://www.nationalreview.com/kudlows-money-politics/2072/washington-going-wrong-way, accessed January 2, 2013.

2. Rob Davies, "China becomes world's leading car manufacturer with purchase of Volvo from Ford for £1.2billion," *Daily Mail*, March 29, 2010, http://www.dailymail.co.uk/news/article-1261404/China-worlds-leading-car-manufacturer-purchase-Volvo-Ford-1-2billion.html, accessed January 6, 2013.

3. "2012 Index of Economic Freedom," New York: Heritage Foundation, 2012, http://www.heritage.org/index/country/china, accessed January 2, 2013.

4. Zhang Hong, "One-Child Policy Is Harming China," *Economic Observer*, May 9, 2012, http://www.eeo.com.cn/ens/2012/0509/226124.shtml, accessed January 2, 2013.

5. Keith Fitz-Gerald, "Jim Rogers: China's Economic Advance Is All but Unstoppable," *Money Morning*, April 15, 2008, http://moneymorning. com/2008/04/15/jim-rogers-chinas-economic-advance-is-all-but-unstoppable/, accessed January 2, 2013.

6. Sunil Asnani, "Assessing India and China," AdvisorAnalyst.com, March 18, 2010, http://advisoranalyst.com/glablog/2010/03/18/assessing-india-and-china/, accessed January 2, 2013.

7. Vikas Jajaj and Jim Yardley, "Scandal Poses a Riddle: Will India Ever Be Able to Tackle Corruption?," *New York Times*, September 15, 2012, http://www .nytimes.com/2012/09/16/world/asia/scandal-bares-corruption-hampering-indias-growth.html?pagewanted=all&_r=0, accessed January 2, 2013.

8. Elliott R. Morss, "China and India: Is Either a Good Bet?," SeekingAlpha .com, August 29, 2012, http://seekingalpha.com/article/836451-china-and-india-is-either-a-good-bet, accessed January 2, 2013.

9. "2012 Index of Economic Freedom," New York: Heritage Foundation, 2012, http://www.heritage.org/index/country/india, accessed January 2, 2013.

10. Sunil Asnani, "Assessing India and China," AdvisorAnalyst.com, March 18, 2010, http://advisoranalyst.com/glablog/2010/03/18/assessing-india-and-china/, accessed January 2, 2013.

11. Nicholas Vardy, http://www.nicholasvardy.com/global-guru/articles/the-asian-tigers-revisited-part-1/.

12. November 14, 2011 whitehouse.gov http://www.whitehouse.gov/the-press-office/2011/11/14/news-conference-president-obama.

13. "2012 Index of Economic Freedom," New York: Heritage Foundation, 2012, http://www.heritage.org/index/, accessed January 2, 2013.

14. Andrew Burrell, "Chinese Mining Executive Would Rather Invest in Australia's Agriculture to Meet China's Food Demand," *Australian*, July 17, 2012, http://www.theaustralian.com.au/business/economics/chinese-mining-executive-would-rather-invest-in-australias-agriculture-to-meet-chinas-food-demand/story-e6frg926-1226427550181, accessed January 2, 2013.

15. Grant Powell, Vedrana Savic, and Amy Chng, "Destination South East Asia: A Joint Pathway to Future Growth? Opportunities for Regional Business Expansion," Accenture, http://www.accenture.com/Microsites/ management-consulting-innovation-center/Documents/pdf/Accenture-Opportunities-for-Regional-Business-Expansion.pdf, accessed January 2, 2013.

16. Anthony Fensom, "Forget Europe: Is the Real Debt Crisis in Japan?," *Diplomat*, October 30, 2012, http://thediplomat.com/2012/10/30/japan-land-of-the-rising-debt/, accessed January 2, 2013.

17. Phone interview with J. J. Sussman, January 4, 2013.

18. Seth Zalkin, interview.

19. Gail Moss, "Latin America: No More Stereotypes," *Investment and Pensions Europe*, January 3, 2012, http://www.ipe.com/magazine/latin-america-no-more-stereotypes_43533.php, accessed January 7, 2013.

20. Jason Voss, CFA, "6 Myths About Investing in Africa," SeekingAlpha.com, March 14, 2012, http://seekingalpha.com/article/433301-6-myths-about-investing-in-africa, accessed January 2, 2013.

21. Ibid.

22. Natasha Gural, "Investing in Europe's Fastest-Growing Economy," CNBC .com, August 15, 2012, http://www.cnbc.com/id/48552347/page/2/, accessed January 2, 2013.

23. Dmitry Sedov, "Turkey Headed for Trouble," *Strategic Culture Foundation*, April 9, 2012, http://www.strategic-culture.org/news/2012/09/04/turkey-headed-for-trouble.html, accessed January 2, 2013.

24. "Moody's Reviews 6 Canadian Banks for Downgrade," CBC News, October 26, 2012, http://www.cbc.ca/news/business/story/2012/10/26/moodys-banks-credit-review.html, accessed January 2, 2013.

25. The Dividend Guy, "Canadian Banks Are Among the Most Solid In the World," SeekingAlpha.com, November 21, 2012, http://seekingalpha.com/article/1022591-canadian-banks-are-among-the-most-solid-in-the-world, accessed January 2, 2013.

26. Tawhid Ali, "Are European Value Stocks Poised for Recovery?," *Alliance Bernstein Blog on Investing*, October 25, 2012, http://blog.alliancebernstein .com/index.php/2012/10/25/are-european-value-stocks-poised-for-recovery/, accessed January 2, 2013.

Chapter 5

1. Securities and Exchange Commission, http://www.sec.gov/investor/pubs/ininvest.htm.

2. Personal correspondence, December 11, 2012.

3. Jeremy Schwartz and Christopher Gannatti, "The Case for Small Cap Earnings," WisdomTree, no publication date, http://www.wisdomtree .com/elqNow/elqRedir.htm?ref=http://www.wisdomtree.com/resource-library/pdf/whitepapers/WisdomTree-Case-for-SmallCap-Earnings-794 .pdf, accessed January 7, 2013.

4. Jason Zweig, "How Many Stocks Should You Own? The Answer Is a Lot More, and a Lot Fewer, than You Probably Think," CNNMoney, September 11, 2007, http://money.cnn.com/2007/09/06/pf/zweig_september.moneymag/index.htm, accessed January 7, 2013.

5. Roger Nusbaum, "Anything Can Go to Zero," Seeking Alpha, April 20, 2012, http://seekingalpha.com/article/513911-anything-can-go-to-zero, accessed January 7, 2013.

Chapter 6

1. Douglas J. Peebles, "Global Bonds: Protection in Down Markets," AllianceBernstein website, July 25, 2012, http://blog.alliancebernstein .com/index.php/2012/07/25/global-bonds-protection-in-down-markets/, accessed January 7, 2013.
2. E-mail interview, October 17, 2012.
3. Ian Salisbury "ETFs Were Wider Off the Mark in 2009," *Wall Street Journal,* February 19, 2010, http://online.wsj.com/article/NA_WSJ_PUB :SB10001424052748704269004575073850786749116.html, accessed January 7, 2013.
4. Tom Lydon, "Emerging Market Bond ETFs: Looking Overseas for Yield," Seeking Alpha, October 29, 2012, http://seekingalpha.com/article/959771-emerging-market-bond-etfs-looking-overseas-for-yield, accessed January 7, 2013.
5. Terry Pristin, "A Closer, and Skeptical, Look at Nontraded REITs," *New York Times,* (July 19, 2011, http://www.nytimes.com/2011/07/20/realestate/ commercial/nontraded-reits-face-increased-scrutiny, accessed January 3, 2013.
6. FundersClub, EarlyShares, and OurCrowd are crowdfunding leaders at the time this book is being written, but things move quickly in technology.

Chapter 7

1. Nick Hodge, "No-Spin Investment Ideas: Tune Out the Noise," *Wealth Daily,* November 2, 2012, http://www.wealthdaily.com/articles/no-spin-investment-ideas/3752, accessed January 7, 2013.
2. David K. Randall, "The Average Investor Is His Own Worst Enemy," *Forbes,* June 28, 2012, http://www.forbes.com/forbes/2010/0628/investment-guide-behaviorial-finance-odean-average-investor-own-enemy_2.html, accessed January 7, 2013.
3. Interview with Covestor CEO Asheesh Advani, December 7, 2012.

Index

About the Authors

Aaron Katsman is the founder and president of Lighthouse Capital Ltd., a boutique investment firm serving a global clientele. Lighthouse Capital offers securities through Portfolio Resources Group, Inc., a registered broker-dealer that is a member of FINRA, SIPC, MSRB, and SIFMA. He also writes a popular weekly investment column for the *Jerusalem Post*. Katsman has been a guest on CNBC's *Squawk Box* and contributes to Seeking Alpha. He is the author of the investment blog www.gpsinvestor.com.

Aaron was born in Seattle, Washington, and holds a BA in political science from Yeshiva University in New York. He moved to Israel in 1992. He founded and managed the international personal banking group for Citigroup in Israel. Prior to Citigroup, he was a senior analyst at a leading Israeli venture capital fund, where he gained an intimate working knowledge of the Israeli high-tech industry and was frequently invited to lecture on the Israeli economy. He is licensed by the Israel Securities Authority and holds the following registrations with FINRA and the SEC in the United States: General Securities Representative Examination (Series 7); Uniform Securities Agent State Law Examination (Series 63); Uniform Investment Adviser Law Examination (Series 65).

Aaron is married with five children, and when he is not working or volunteering, he enjoys running half-marathons. When back in Seattle, he tries to catch "the" elusive king salmon.

Tamela Rich is a business writer based in Charlotte, North Carolina, where she lives with her family. As a manuscript consultant and ghostwriter of books, presentations, and articles for executives, she was delighted to collaborate with Aaron on this project. She earned her MBA at the Fuqua School of Business at Duke University.

Her first book, *Live Full Throttle: Life Lessons from Friends Who Faced Cancer* (2012), won three national book awards. Her second book, *Lean into Life: Lessons from the Road,* will be published in October 2013.